The Sermon On the Mount
Jesus Christ Commands His Disciples

ISBN 978-1-7330564-7-2 (Paper Back)
Book Design and Authorship by Don Pirozok
Editor Cheryl Pirozok

First Printing 2021 Amazon Publishing, United States

Published By: Pilgrims Progress Publishing
Spokane Valley WA. 99206
Website: www.donpirozok.com

Sermon On the Mount
Jesus Christ Commands His Disciples

Table of Contents

Introduction pg. 3

Chapter 1 The Beatitudes pg. 11

Chapter 2 Persecuted For Righteousness pg. 54

Chapter 3 Warnings of Losing the Kingdom pg. 73

Chapter 4 Lusting After Women pg. 83

Chapter 5 Practical Acts pg. 99

Chapter 6 Giving To God and Heavenly Treasure pg. 107

Chapter 7 Seeking First the Kingdom pg. 121

Chapter 8 Heavenly Treasures and Rewards pg. 146

Chapter 9 Judge Not, That You Be Judged pg. 167

Chapter 10 The Narrow Way pg. 180

Chapter 11 The Peril of the False Prophets pg. 198

Conclusion pg. 220

The Sermon On the Mount
Jesus Christs Commands For His Disciples

Introduction

Jesus Sermon To His Disciples

Matthew 5:1-2

1 And seeing the multitudes, he went up into a mountain: and when he was set, his disciples came unto him:
2 And he opened his mouth, and taught them, saying,

The Sermon On the Mount

When Jesus Christ had called His disciples, He went up into a Mountain and gave what is called the Sermon On the Mount in Scriptures. What Jesus taught is recorded in three chapters by the Apostle Matthew. The Sermon On the Mount is considered a mini version of the Christian faith, with Christs commands to His disciples. Its significance is in defining characteristics of living fully for Jesus Christ as a true disciple of the Lord. The Sermon On the Mount is in considerable contrast to the ways and values of the world system. For this reason, many are they which name the name of the Lord, and fewer are they which follow His commands.

The Sermon On the Mount makes it especially difficult for its challenges and commands teaching the necessity of obedience to Jesus Christ. Many teachers have attempted to teach the Sermon On the Mount is for Jews of that day only. Or the Sermon was only for Jewish Christians during the time of Christ until He went to the Cross. After which the commands given in the Sermon which were thought to be related to the Old Testament and giving of the law. Now the law gave way to the Gospel of Grace, this is true. However, the Sermon On the Mount could never be fulfilled by any man except by the grace of Christ. This makes the Sermon On the Mount as applicable today for all true disciples in Christ, as it was given to Christs original disciples. The Sermon On the Mount is New Testament teaching given by Christ for all authentic disciples.

The Sermon On the Mount is broken down into many portions but all point to a life of complete surrender as a disciple of Jesus Christ. Some of the more notable characteristics given in the Sermon On the Mount are called the Beatitudes. These characteristics are what define true disciples of Jesus Christ and are what separate the saints for the rest of the world. As the born-again saint has a new nature with the indwelling Holy Spirit. This gives Christians a new heart and new spirit, with the ability to keep the commands given by the Lord in the Sermon On the Mount. The new nature with the indwelling Spirit gives the born-again disciple of Christ the ability to keep the commandments of the Beatitudes. Without Christ indwelling keeping the character of the Beatitudes would be impossible. As all these commands are so contrary to the world system, no man outside of Christ would never want to sacrifice his life in order to obey these directives.

Another thing to consider is the cost in obeying the commands of Christ. Not only must the disciple of Jesus Christ lay down his life, the true discile in following the Lord will suffer persecution. All these realities are given in the Sermon On the Mount. The cost of following the Lord is clearly spelled out in the Sermon. Which leads to the potential failure of many Christians who refuse to pay that cost. Many examples of potential compromise are given by the Lord, and the ultimate cost of not fulfilling the demands are given in warnings to everyone who would be the Lord's disciple. Understanding the loss involved is a big part of the Sermon On the Mount, therefore many Christians are tempted to flee from the warnings of judgment. Many Christians are wanting to say the Cross has resolved all conflicts with God, as the Cross has provided the free gift of grace. No man can add to or take away from the grace of salvation which Christ alone has purchased by the Cross. However, the Sermon On the Mount speaks towards conditional promises based upon meeting certain conditions. These conditions are not about earning our salvation, instead are the conditions given to the already saved to qualify for the coming Kingdom of Heaven age. The judgment at the end of the Sermon On the Mount are not the loss of eternal life, instead are the loss of entering the Kingdom of Heaven age.

So, when considering the righteousness of God in Christ as provided by the Cross and Resurrection, we must keep the blood Sacrifice as perfect. Meeting every demand of sinless perfection, Christ is the Lamb of God who is without spot or blemish. An everlasting Sacrifice which can never be corrupted which meets all the demands of a Holy perfect God. This righteousness is part and parcel of the righteous which comes from the Cross and the sinless Son of God Jesus Christ. The blood sacrifice of Jesus Christ has paid for our eternal redemption in full. What is measured in the Sermon On the Mount are works of righteousness after coming into saving faith. As the Cross has already judged our sin and given us complete justification in the eyes of God. However, every Christian must appear at the Judgment Seat of Christ to have their works judged for reward or loss of reward.

So, the other kind of righteousness, the righteous acts of the saints will be judged. We have already been declared holy, and blameless irreprovable in His sight. Now we must walk out our salvation with fear and trembling for it is Christ who works in you to will and do according to His good pleasure. This righteousness is not accredited by the Cross, instead are the righteous acts of the saints after coming into saving faith. The judgment which all in Christ must experience is at the Second Coming of Jesus Christ and is called the Judgment Seat of Christ. What is judged are our acts of righteousness which will qualify us for entrance into the Kingdom of Heaven. For those who did not obey the Lord who did not follow the commands of the Sermon On the Mount, are in danger of disqualification. A warning of Christians not inheriting the Kingdom of Heaven. Their Salvation is not measured, instead their works after coming into saving faith. Rewards given or taken away related to the Kingdom of heaven age.

The Beatitudes Are Like the 10 Commandments

Moses went up on Mount Sinai which burned with fire as the Lord had descended there. Upon the Mountain of God Moses was given the 10 commandments which defined the moral relationship Israel was to have with God. The commandments are a source and guide as to the nature and character of God for in keeping them a man will be blessed and not cursed. Sadly, the fallen nature of man only proves man's inability to keep the commandments, as the result fallen man resides under the wrath of God. The law of the commandments are without respect of persons for In breaking Gods laws we sow to destruction and come under the curse of the law.

When Jesus Christ came, He took his disciples upon a mountain and gave the Beatitudes. How different are these characteristics from the way the average person lives upon the earth? Do we realize in order to live as a disciple of Jesus Christ we must follow the Beatitudes which the Lord gave as the character of His life? Also notice when a disciple does not follow the way of the Beatitudes, he must forfeit the future rewards promised in them.

Notice the poor in spirit is given the Kingdom of heaven. The poor are trampled upon by the ambitious of this age. So many Christians are proclaiming they possesses the kingdom when they are unwilling to be last in order to receive it. In reality they build a kingdom after their own image and not after the character of Jesus Christ.

Those who mourn now are comforted then. Mourning requires the fellowship of the Lord's sufferings. Few are they who are willing to pick up the Cross to follow after the Lord. Without suffering for Jesus Christ, you cannot inherit the coming Kingdom of Heaven. So many have embraced a Cross less Christianity which does not have the character of the Lord.

Blessed are the meek for they shall inherit the earth. Great are the mighty men who seek to run the world. Ever attempting to establish their will and way. The meek have laid down their agenda to follow the will of the Lord. To them is given the reward of ruling and reigning with Christ in the Kingdom age. For it is the meek who are given charge over the earth, not the proud and lofty.

Blessed are they who do hunger for righteousness. How close to the world do many Christians live. For those who will not love the world have separated from the world unto God in a holy life. At the resurrection of the righteous they will be filled with the reward of a righteous holy life.

Blessed are the merciful for they shall obtain mercy. How necessary is the act of forgiveness with the merciful? How can a Saint inherit the next age when they are not willing to forgive the sin of others, and Christ died to forgive all their sins? Holding on to the sins of others is the source of great bondage in the lives of the human race. By the grace of God, we extend mercy when we forgive, lest holding on to sin we see the root of bitterness choke out the love of Christ.

Only the pure in heart will stand in the congregation of the just on the Day of Judgment. For the blessed and holy are they who will partake in the first resurrection. For the rest of the dead must wait one thousand years before they are raised in the second resurrection. The pure in heart will see God's justice and will rule with the Lord in the next age. Those who are impure will be shut out and not see the Lord. "Depart from Me you workers of iniquity for I never knew you." (Matthew 7:23)

The peacemakers are called God's children. For the world is at war with God and with one another. The sons of God are revealed at the end of this age. Not all will qualify for the stature of a mature son who is qualified to rule with Christ. Those who walked with the Lord trusting in the blood of Jesus Christ, as the only true way to have peace with God. Confessing their own sins and being quick to forgive the sins of others. In this way the sons of God can grow up in the grace and stature of the Lord. These are the sons who will be revealed in glory at the Second Coming of Jesus Christ.

Matthew 5:1-12
1 And seeing the multitudes, he went up into a mountain: and when he was set, his disciples came unto him:
2 And he opened his mouth, and taught them, saying,
3 Blessed are the poor in spirit: for theirs is the kingdom of heaven.
4 Blessed are they that mourn: for they shall be comforted.
5 Blessed are the meek: for they shall inherit the earth.
6 Blessed are they which do hunger and thirst after righteousness: for they shall be filled.
7 Blessed are the merciful: for they shall obtain mercy.
8 Blessed are the pure in heart: for they shall see God.
9 Blessed are the peacemakers: for they shall be called the children of God.
10 Blessed are they which are

persecuted for righteousness' sake: for theirs is the kingdom of heaven.
11 Blessed are ye, when men shall
revile you, and persecute you, and shall say all manner of evil against you falsely, for my sake.
12 Rejoice, and be exceeding
glad: for great is your reward in heaven: for so persecut ed they the prophets which were before you.

Chapter One
The Beatitudes

Blessed Are the Poor in Spirit

Matthew 5:3
3 Blessed are the poor in spirit: for theirs is the kingdom of heaven.

Who are the poor in Spirit? The prophet Isaiah gives some understanding who the poor in spirit are as considered by God.
Isiah 66:1-2
 1 Thus saith the Lord, The heaven is my throne, and the earth is my footstool: where is **house that** unto me? and where is the place of my rest?
2 For all those things hath mine hand made, and all those things have been, saith the Lord: but to
this man will I look, even to him that is poor and of a contrite spirit, and trembleth at my word.

Perhaps the poor in spirit are those of Christ who know God is in control. Even though all circumstances would say otherwise. The poor in spirit never lose their trust in God. Especially, those who break before the Lord, and are contrite who are living in the fear of the Lord and tremble at His word. The poor in the Spirit are not trying to improve the world, are not exercising their will in kingdom building. Instead see the promise of kingdom future and walking by faith through this present evil age as a pilgrim on a journey towards the Second Coming of Jesus Christ.

The Sermon On the Mount teaches Christ's disciples how to seek first the Kingdom of Heaven. In contrast to the rich and powerful who want to control the world, the poor in Spirit are the true inheritors of the Kingdom age. The right to rule and reign on earth with Jesus Christ at the Second Coming. The Kingdom of Heaven is the government of Jesus Christ on earth for one thousand years. It commences after the Great Tribulation and the defeat of Antichrist and his armies in the Battle of Armageddon which ends this present evil age. The powerful men, the rich, and the kings of the earth will hide in dens, and in caves from the wrath of God when Christ returns to judge and make war.

Isaiah 2:10-12
10 Enter into the rock, and hide thee in the dust, for fear of the Lord, and for the glory of his majesty.

11 The lofty looks of man shall be humbled, and the
haughtiness of men shall be bowed down, and
the Lord alone shall be exalted in that day.
12 For the day of the Lord of hosts shall be upon
every one that is proud and lofty, and upon every one
that is lifted up; and he shall be brought low:

The kings of the earth have joined themselves with the
Antichrist to rule the entire world. This has been in part
the practice of every world dictator, men who exalt
themselves as little gods over the earth. However, the
way of the saints is the opposite spirit, to be poor in
Spirit speaks of being in need because of serving and
giving their lives to Jesus Christ. A disciple of Jesus Christ
is required to pick up the Cross in self-denial to
fellowship in the sufferings of Jesus Christ. Christ's
disciples are to have the mind of Christ considering the
needs of others more important than their own. The
way of inheriting the Kingdom age is through loss in this
present evil age. In seeking first, the coming kingdom
age, the saints are to lay treasures in heaven and not
build their own kingdoms now.

Of late Church has been tempted by a false Gospel
which teaches the Church is the kingdom on earth and
is to take over the world before Jesus Christ can return.
What is the problem? You must exploit the Church and
amass wealth and riches, and you must position
yourself over others to gain a following and audience. In
essence you must build a following which requires a

degree of self-exaltation, and self-promotion. In the end men will have their eyes on you and exalt you into a position which God has never intended. A false reputation, a false image must be built and sustained. In the end you are allowing men to lift you up in their eyes which leads to the glorification of men.

In the authentic world of apostles, and prophets of God there is shame and reproach, and even martyrdom. The apostles of the Lord were considered fools for Christ, the least, the off scouring of the earth. A true apostle of Christ will suffer in the fellowship of Christ's sufferings, which greatly damages the pride of man. In seeking first, the Kingdom of Heaven wealth and riches, and pride and ego of man are sacrificed in service of Jesus Christ.

What does a multimillionaire apostle get at the Judgment Seat of Christ? The exalted rich man gets to see all his wealth and worldly riches burn up as wood, hay, and stubble. How hard will it be for a rich man to enter the kingdom of heaven. It will easier for a camel to go through the eye of the needle than for a rich man to enter the kingdom of Heaven age. As they have exploited the Church to build their kingdom on earth, they are excluded from ruling with Jesus Christ in the millennium. The poor in spirit pass through the judicial fires as they do not have the worlds wealth, riches, and fame. Instead, their works the world despised, as it brought glory to the Lord and not their own lives. Hardly can a rich man be made poor in Spirit. Selling all now of his earthly treasure becoming poor, only to be made rich with the Lord at the Second Coming. How the lowly are looked down upon, but theirs is the kingdom of heaven.

1 Corinthians 3:9-23
9 For we are labourers together with God: ye are God's husbandry, ye are God's building.
10 According to the grace of God which is given unto me, as a wise master builder, I have laid the foundation, and another buildeth thereon. But let every man take heed how he buildeth thereupon.
11 For other foundation can no man lay than that is laid, which is Jesus Christ.
12 Now if any man build upon this foundation gold, silver, precious sto nes, wood, hay, stubble;
13 Every man's work shall be made manifest: for the day shall declare it, because revealed by fire; and the fire shall try every man's work of what sort it is.
14 If any man's work abide which he hath built thereupon, he shall receive a reward.
15 If any man's work shall be burned, he shall suffer loss: but he himself shall be saved; yet so as by fire.
16 Know ye not that ye are the temple of God, and that the Spirit of God dwelleth in you?
17 If any man defile the temple of God, him shall God destroy; for the temple of God is holy, which temple ye are.
18 Let no man deceive himself. If any man among you seemeth to be wise in this world, let

him become a fool, that he may be wise.
19 For the wisdom of
this world is foolishness with God. For it is written, He
taketh the wise in their own craftiness.
20 And again, The Lord knoweth the thoughts of the
wise, that they are vain.
21 Therefore let no man glory in men. For all
things are yours;
22 Whether Paul, or Apollos, or Cephas, or the
world, or life, or death, or things present, or things to
come; all are yours;
23 And ye are Christ's; and Christ is God's.

Blessed Are They Who Mourn
Matthew 5:4
4 Blessed are they that mourn: for they shall be
comforted.

Why would Jesus Christ teach the mourning disciples
are blessed of the Lord? The apostle John can give us
some insights into the matter.

John 16:20-22
20 Verily, verily, I say unto you, That ye shall
weep and lament, but the world shall rejoice: and yes
shall be sorrowful, but your sorrow shall be
turned into joy.
21 A woman when she is in
travail hath sorrow, because her hour is come: but as
soon as she is delivered of the child, she

remembereth no more the anguish, for joy that a man is born into the world.
22 And ye now therefore have sorrow: but I will
see you again, and your heart shall rejoice, and your joy no man taketh from you.

Here are we given a contrast between the disciples of Christ and the rest of the world. When the disciples were eyewitness to the Crucifixion of Jesus Christ their dreams for the restoration of the Kingdom to Israel were dashed and broken. Image for three years they believed Jesus Christ to be the prophesied Son of David who would deliver Israel from foreign occupation. Making Israel the head of nations once again. Jesus Christ warned His disciples a time of weeping, sorrow, and lamenting was just ahead. However, with the resurrection of Jesus Christ their sorrow would be turned to joy. So, it is for the disciples today, with the Lord away our time is like the wilderness walk of faith. The difficulty of trials and testing that must accompany the saints in this present evil age. We are like the pregnant women who carries the burden of the Lord, but when the time of our deliverance from this age has come our mourning will be turned to absolute joy. As the apostle has spoken these present sufferings will be nothing to be compared to the glory to be revealed in us at the Second Coming of the Lord.

The hardship of the Christian life is spelled out in the Sermon On the Mount. All who live a Godly life as a disciple of Jesus Christ will walk through this present evil age as a pilgrim, a sojourner knowing this world is not our home. While we are present in this mortal body, we are absent from the Lord. Meaning we await the Day of our Redemption, which happens in the first resurrection to the righteous just in the Lord. It will be at this time our morning will be turned to joy. As the Lord has promised eye has not seen, nor has ear heard, or has entered into the heart of man the things which God has prepared for those who love Him.

True disciples in the Lord carry the burden of the Lord in this age. We are the Light and Salt of the earth which are agents which preserve against corruption. The true disciples of the Lord will morn over their sin, the sin of others, and the basic corruption in the nations. No disciple who has given himself in obedience can enjoy his sin, for he mourns the loss of true fellowship in the Light, until by confession and repentance He is restored to true fellowship with the Lord once again.

Mourning Over A Fallen World

James 4:4-9

[4] Ye adulterers and adulteresses, know ye not that the friendship of the world is enmity with God? whosoever therefore will be a friend of the world is the enemy of God.

[5] Do ye think that the scripture saith in vain, The spirit that dwelleth in us lusteth to envy?

[6] But he giveth more grace. Wherefore he saith, God resisteth the proud, but giveth grace unto the humble.

[7] Submit yourselves therefore to God. Resist the devil, and he will flee from you.   [8] Draw nigh to God, and he will draw nigh to you. Cleanse your hands, ye sinners; and purify your hearts, ye double minded. [9] Be afflicted, and mourn, and weep: let your laughter be turned to mourning, and your joy to heaviness.

The Disciple of Christ is considered a pilgrim on a journey towards the Second Coming of Jesus Christ. This present evil age is not the home of the born-again child of God. The danger of stopping your pilgrimage, and loving the world is noted throughout the New Testament. The apostle James speaks of saint's friendship with the world is to make one an enemy of God. Why is this so important? Christians live in a God hating world where sin and darkness are loved by those who reject Jesus Christ. The true saint of God will be broken before God and mourn over the sin loving, God hating world.

The Scriptures reveal God will not allow any other gods before Him. As those who love the world provokes the Lord by His indwelling Holy Spirit. You cannot love the world and live a life of sin for it will deeply grieve the Holy Spirit. A disciple of Jesus Christ will mourn over his sin and will mourn over the world's enmity with God.

God will resist any who call upon His name who wants to adulterate with the world. God will give more grace to the humble who are broken over the world. God resists those who will not mourn now, who have lost themselves to the love of the things of the world. The Lord requires His disciples to draw near, making for a purification, cleansing our hands, and purifying out hearts. This purification of the world, and from sin will break the saint before God. Mourning over our struggles for sanctification before God will be a reality for all who truly obey the commands of Jesus Christ.

As the Scriptures are inspired by God, all which the apostle James has written are in accord with the Sermon On the Mount. Be afflicted and mourn now so the disciple of Christ can be comforted then with the return of the Lord. Let your laughter be turned to mourning as you suffer the loss of the worlds influences over your life. However, mourning now will be led to being comforted with Kingdom age inheritance in the future.

The Meek Shall Inherit the Earth

Matthew 5:5
5 Blessed are the meek: for they shall inherit the earth.

The meek are called to suffer injustice patiently. The meek are to inherit the earth. Why? The meek at this time do not enjoy at present the power, riches, and happiness of the earth. As the possessors of the world have not the love of God. The saints are called upon to wait for the Lord to establish His justice upon the earth, upon the rule of the Kingdom of heaven on earth at the Second Coming of Jesus Christ.

With all the political battles and real time wars going on throughout the entire world one might wonder what will happen in the future. Jesus Christ predicted the rise of wars and rumors of wars with nation rising against nation, and kingdom against kingdom. The fallen nature of man lends towards bloodshed by war, and world history has proven this a fact. Right now, in American politics we see a great deal of evil plotting by men and women who think it their right to rule the masses. The world is changing rapidly as philosophical beliefs are being pushed down our throats on how to govern, and all manner of corruption in morality is being made into law.

Standing in contrast to the world is Jesus Christ, and the disciples of Jesus Christ. Jesus Christ was portrayed as a Lamb to slaughter who did not resist those who spit and beat upon him. Those who mocked and railed upon the Creator of Heaven and earth. Jesus Christ did not fight with legions of angels to establish His Kingdom on earth, Christ did not attempt to overthrow Rome. Upon the Cross Jesus Christ proclaimed Father forgive them for they do not know what they do. Jesus demonstrated meekness in His Crucifixion and was willing to be obedient unto death even the death of the Cross.

What has happened to modern organized Christianity? The loss of Christ' character, in the place of Christ likeness is all manner of man's character, and the worlds pride. The modern Church has lost the character of Christ's meekness, the poor in spirit are no longer of any value in the eyes of the modern Church. Where is the Cross of Jesus Christ in the minds of modern Christians? Where is the self-denial the picking up of the Cross to fellowship in the sufferings of Jesus Christ? Where is the knowledge of Christ making disciples which are least in the eyes of the world? Fools for Christ in this present evil age, afterwards are glorified with Christ in the Kingdom age? Hardly can a man choose the straight and narrow path which leads a man from building his own kingdom. Those who seek fame and glory from this present evil age, who use the Church to make a profit and a name.

Why is the modern Church caught up into politics? It has become a vain substitute to fill up the void left by the abandonment of the Cross. Men who are play acting they can change the world by their genius, will, and charm. Politics has become a noble reason for Christians to make for a better world. Standing up for the truth has not become standing up for Jesus Christ, instead it has committed all manner of zeal and proclamation for one's favorite politician. If Jesus Christ had wanted to save the world through politics, He would have displayed Himself as a Great Commander, a world leader, and Great King to rule the nations. Instead,

Christ made Himself of no reputation was born a slave to die. Those who serve the Lord are Christ's slaves and are considered worthless, preaching the foolishness of the Cross.

The compromised Church has charmed itself with the world's riches. Saying we are great men, world conquers, who are rich and in need of nothing. Being self-sufficient the compromised Church does not depend upon the Lord of Glory anymore, and have left Him outside off the organized Church knocking on the door to get in. Hearts are filled with pride and self-promotion and filling up the Church will vain proclamations which allure through the lusts of the flesh. Starlite eyes blinded by reason of the worlds images which many have fallen down to worship. The discipline of the loss of all things so we might gain Christ is despised, instead we must show the world how rich and capable we are. Being stripped of the character of Christ, we are no longer clothed with meekness and we have become blind to our own nakedness. The compromised Church have really become somebody in our own eyes, not realizing we stand before God as blind, miserable, and naked. The Church without meekness, without being pour in spirit has lost the light and salt. The modern Church of man-made glory is in danger of being cast out and trodden underfoot by man.

What is the outcome then? Men of fame, and great political leaders will not inherit. For the Kingdom of

Heaven will come in due time. All those who take the Cross now will wear the Crown then. It is not the proud man who will possess the Kingdom. It is not the mighty man, instead the meek will inherit the earth. Blessed are the poor in Spirit for theirs is the Kingdom of Heaven.

Isaiah 53
Who hath believed our report? and to whom is the arm of the Lord revealed?
2 For he shall grow up before him as a tender plant, and as a root out of a dry ground: he hath no form nor comeliness; and when we shall see him, there is no beauty that we should desire him.
3 He is despised and rejected of men; a man of sorrows, and acquainted with grief: and we hid as it were our faces from him; he was despised, and we esteemed him not.
4 Surely he hath borne our griefs, and carried our sorrows: yet we did esteem him stricken, smitten of God, and afflicted.
5 But he was wounded for our transgressions, he was bruised for our iniquities: the chastisement of our peace was upon him; and with his stripes we are healed.
6 All we like sheep have gone astray; we have turned everyone to his own way; and the Lord hath laid on him the iniquity of us all.
7 He was oppressed, and he was afflicted, yet he opened not his mouth: he is brought as a lamb to the slaughter, and as a sheep before her shearers is

dumb, so he openeth not his mouth.

8 He was taken from prison and from judgment: and who shall declare his generation? for he was cut off out of the land of the living: for the transgression of my people was he stricken.

9 And he made his grave with the wicked, and with the rich in his death; because he had done no violence, neither was any deceit in his mouth.

10 Yet it pleased the Lord to bruise him; he hath put him to grief: when thou shalt make his soul an offering for sin, he shall see his seed, he shall prolong his days, and the pleasure of the Lord shall prosper in his hand.

11 He shall see of the travail of his soul, and shall be satisfied: by his knowledge shall my righteous servant justify many; for he shall bear their iniquities.

12 Therefore will I divide him a portion with the great, and he shall divide the spoil with the strong; because he hath poured out his soul unto death: and he was numbered with the transgressors; and he bare the sin of many, and made intercession for the transgressors.

Matthew 5:6
Blessed are they who hunger and thirst after righteousness; for they shall be filled.

In Scriptures two kinds of righteousness are featured. One is the righteousness of God in Christ given a part of the free gift of grace through the Cross of Jesus Christ.

The righteousness of God is sinless perfection which meets the demands of Gods holiness and justice. The Lord Jesus Christ the spotless sinless Son of God tempted in every point as we, yet completely without sin. Christ committed no sin, instead was made to be sin for us, a sin sacrifice to pay the debt to sin which no man could every pay. Christ then through the Cross has been for us the righteousness of God. Therefore, if man be in Christ, he has become a new creation. For He who knew no sin was made to be sin for us, that we might be made the righteousness of God in Him.
(1 Corinthians 5:21). This kind of righteousness is not attained by any human effort or merit. Christ alone was able to fulfill the righteous requirements of the law. Any man who calls upon the name of the Lord will have Christ made unto him righteousness, both in satisfying God's justice and by a new nature which is free from being a slave to sin.

The Second kind of righteousness comes from the first kind but is not the free gift instead is the righteousness of the saints. This kind of righteousness comes from works of faith after coming into saving faith.

James 2:20-25
20 But wilt
thou know, O vain man, that faith without works is dead
21 Wasnot Abraham our father justified by works, when he had offered Isaac his son upon the altar?
22 Seest thou how faith wrought

with his works, and by works was faith made perfect?
23 And the scripture was fulfilled which
saith, Abraham believed God, and it was imputed unto
him for righteousness: and he was called the Friend of
God.
24 Ye see then how that by works a man is
justified, and not by faith only.
25 Likewise also was not Rahab the
harlot justified by works, when she had received the
messengers, and had sent them out another way?
26 For as the body without the
spirit is dead, so faith without works is dead also.

The second kind of righteousness comes from works
which Jesus Christ will measure at the Judgment Seat
for rewards, or loss of rewards. Just like Abraham's faith
in God led him to offer Isaac as a blood sacrifice was
considered a work of righteousness by God. When
Abraham offered Isaac, it was imputed to him for
righteousness by God. You can see how Abraham's faith
worked with obedient actions, and by works was faith
made perfect. Abraham was able to complete his faith
in God by works which come out of a desire to be right
before God.

One kind of righteousness comes from the free gift or
grace, the other kind of righteousness comes from
works of faith in obedience to Christ after coming into
saving faith. As impossible are righteous works of
reward without first having come into saving faith, so

are righteous rewards without works of faith. As the Sermon On the Mount is likened to the commandments of the Lord for His disciples. Those who would want to honor and glorify the Lord with their lives must recognize both kinds of righteousness. The Cross of Jesus Christ which has freed them from slavery to sin, so righteous works in obedience can be rewarded at the Second Coming of Jesus Christ.

As we live in a fallen world of sin and death the Disciples of Jesus Christ are faced with a multitude of trials and tests and trials. A longing for personal holiness coupled with a battle with the world, the flesh, and evil spirits will press the saint of God to purse real freedom in Christ. Many who call themselves Christian will compromise in these trials and are unwilling to pick up the Cross in self-denial, and in the fellowship of the sufferings of Christ. In this present evil age these disciples of Christ must overcome and be zealous for good works.

Jesus Christs teaches; "Blessed are they who hunger and thirst for righteousness for they shall be filled." In this age those who follow the Lord will be filled with the fruit of righteousness which is the internal result of maturing in Christ. The fruit which comes from the Holy Spirit and growth into Christ likeness

.

Philippians 1:9-11
9 And this I pray, that your love may
abound yet more and more in knowledge and in all judg
ment;
10 That ye may approve things that are
excellent; that ye may be sincere and without
offence till the day of Christ;
11 Being filled with the fruits of righteousness, which
are by Jesus Christ, unto the glory and praise of God.

Now the fruits of righteous which would fill our lives can
also extend into the Kingdom of Heaven age. Connected
to works or righteousness is the rewards of
righteousness which can fill our lives in the next age. To
hunger and thirst for righteousness in this age leads to
thirsting for things which would lead the saints to live
right now in this age. For those who are fighting the
good fight off faith, and who are laying hold of eternal
life, their rewards will extend into the next age. For eye
has not seen, nor ear has heard, or has entered into the
heart of man the things which God has prepared for
those who love Him.

We can now understand the warning from the Sermon
On the Mount, "unless your righteousness exceeds the
righteousness of the Scribes and Pharisees, you shall in
no case enter into the Kingdom of heaven." (Matthew
5:20) The righteous of the Scribes and Pharisees are
proven to be hypocrisy. Jesus Christ warns His disciples
against a hypocritical life which does not measure at the

Judgment Seat of Christ. The rest of the Sermon On the Mount is a contrast of righteous works of reward, as compared to religious hypocrisy. The warnings given to Disciples of Christ are very real. For God does not judge a man by respect of persons, instead will judge everyman according to their works. The saints should take the warnings from the Sermon On the Mount teaching as not everyone who calls upon the Lord will enter into the Kingdom of heaven. Blessed are they who in this life did actually hunger and thirst for righteousness, as they will be rewarded with glory in the next age. Even though in this age would require ultimate humiliation.

Blessed Are They Which Hunger and Thirst For Righteousness

Perhaps the connection with sanctification and holiness are implied in this blessing. For those saints who are truly born again of the Holy Spirit, with a new creation man living on the inside a hunger for righteousness is part of the new man in Christ. In this age we know the born-again man has been freed from sins dominion, but still must deal with his flesh, and trails and temptations for a fallen world of sin and corruption. The Scriptures teach even creation groans for the revealing of the sons of God fully freed from sin and corruption. How deep is the cry of the saintly man born of the Spirit who longs and thirsts for righteousness? How can a man born of the Spirit truly commit sin, and be deeply fulfilled with his carnal life? All who thirst for the Lord can truly excuse themselves in sin, being satisfied with an incomplete consecration.

Living a sanctified holy life has promise from God in this present evil age, and for the coming Kingdom age also. Perhaps the beauty of a Christ centered life are the fruits of righteousness. The promise of Gods character filling up the sanctified man who is in true pursuit of Jesus Christ. What are the fruits of righteousness which can fill up a man who hungers for the Lord? The first would be an fulness of God's love, abounding more and more in true knowledge and in all judgment. A man who has grown up spiritually who can know the deeper workings of the Holy Spirit. A man who is moving from faith to faith, strength to strength in Christ, who is able to approve things which are excellent in the Lord. A man approved by the Lord, without guile and pretense being sincere. Without offense till the Day of the Lord. A man kept by the Lord, being filled with fruits of righteousness which come from the Lord. Resulting in glory and praise at the Second Coming of Jesus Christ.

Blessed is the man who hungers for the Lord.

Psalm 42:1-2
1 As the hart panteth after the water brooks, so panteth my soul after thee, O God.
2 My soul thirsteth for God, for the living God: when shall I come and appear before God?

A righteous holy life comes with a special kind of hunger which is given by God Himself. How many newly born again of the Holy Spirit have an insatiable hunger for God. Do you remember when you were newborn of the Spirit, you would devour the Word of God pouring over the Scriptures sometimes for hours, or even days. A hunger and thirst for the Lord comes from being a part of the body of Christ. Those born of the Spirit have Christ's life which is eternal life. Jesus Christ told the woman at the well whosoever drank from Christs living waters would never hunger or thirst no more. Blessed are they who hunger and thirst for the righteous life of Christ for they shall be filled.

John 4:13-14
[13] Jesus answered and said unto her, Whosoever drinketh of this water shall thirst again:
[14] But whosoever drinketh of the water that I shall give him shall never thirst; but the water that I shall give him shall be in him a well of water springing up into everlasting life.

Notice how those who hunger and thirst for Christ are filled with a life which can never pass away or be corrupted. This eternal life in Christ includes Christs promise to raise us out from among the dead. Not only does eternal life satisfy and fulfill our lives now, in the next age Christ will fill our resurrected bodies with His glory. The blessing of hungering for righteousness is given as a reward in the next age by the resurrection and glorification of our lives from mortality into immortality.

John 6:47-51

[47] Verily, verily, I say unto you, He that believeth on me hath everlasting life.

[48] I am that bread of life.

[49] Your fathers did eat manna in the wilderness and are dead.

[50] This is the bread which cometh down from heaven, that a man may eat thereof, and not die.

[51] I am the living bread which came down from heaven: if any man eat of this bread, he shall live forever: and the bread that I will give is my flesh, which I will give for the life of the world.

Christ's promise of being fulfilled when His disciples' hunger and thirst for righteousness, is given as a reward in the first resurrection. Living a holy separated life unto the Lord qualifies His disciples to rule and reign with Christ in the coming Kingdom of Heaven age.

Revelation 20:6

[6] Blessed and holy is he that hath part in the first resurrection: on such the second death hath no power, but they shall be priests of God and of Christ and shall reign with him a thousand years.

Blessed Are the Merciful

Matthew 5:7
Blessed are the merciful, for they shall obtain mercy.

How important for the Dispels of Christ to live from mercy, so they themselves might obtain mercy in judgment.

Blessed Are the Merciful

Mercy is the spirit which is displayed when offenders are in our power : when we might exact our dues and inflict woe upon our enemies. It appears also to include kindness to those in distress.
The law set up justice as its standard. " Justice, justice (marg.) shalt thou follow, that thou mayest live and inherit the land which the Lord thy God giveth thee:" Deut. xvi 20. It bade the Jew use this principle in his dealings with Iris fellows, because that was the principle of God's dealings with himself. It supposed that he rendered to the law all its dues, and it therefore permitted him to exact the same of others.
But the gospel has come in with its cry of * Repentance ! ' It asserts the sinfulness of all It teaches, that only in God's grace is there any hope for transgressors. It bids us, therefore, to use in both our dealings, both with the Church and with the world. The principle upon which we take our stand before God.

The parable of the unmerciful servant is designed to show us the unseemliness of the contrary conduct, and its terrible results, when God shall judge : Matt xviii. 21. And James states the same principle in plain words. " So, speak ye and so do, as they that shall be Judged by the law of liberty. For he shall have judgment without mercy that showed no mercy : mercy rejoiceth against judgment * James ii. 12, 13.

The reason of the blessedness of the merciful is then assigned. " They shall obtain mercy." Of this Psalm xviii. 25 is an ancient witness. " With the merciful thou wilt show Thyself merciful." David found it so. He often spared Saul; he would not put Shimei to death. When he himself is found an offender, he is forgiven: "The Lord also hath put away thy sin: thou shalt not die." Thus, God is pleased to show mercy to the merciful, even here.

But the time for its full display is future. It takes place at the judgment to which Christ will call all His people, a judgment preceding the kingdom. Of this, Paul gives a very clear testimony. "The Lord give mercy to the house of Onesiphobus, for he oft refreshed me, and was not ashamed of my chain. The Lord grant unto him , that he may find mercy of the Lord in that day / " 2 Tim. i. 16 — 18.

" At that day ! " Yes ! mercy will he needed by the saint then, when every deed of his, " whether good or evil," comes before Christ : 2 Cor. v. 10.

Then, Christian, take mercy as your rule. Exact not your debts. " With the same measure that ye measure withal,

it shall be measured to you again. sermon on the
mount expounded. 15
Forgive those that offend against you ! Show kindness
to the feeble, the sick, the aged. "Blessed are the
merciful : for they shall obtain mercy."
As a consequence of this, it seems clear, that no
Christian ought to be a lawyer, or a magistrate, a
member of the army, or the navy. For all these are
different forms of the carrying out of the principle of
justice, and not of mercy.

(The Sermon On the Mount Expounded pages 13-15
Robert Govett)

Exact Not Your Debuts, the temptation is to take justice
into our hands when seeking retribution with our
offenders. How difficult is it in a fallen world of sin,
hatred, and evil not to seek our own vengeance?
Leaving punishment in the hands of God is an act of
mercy by disciples of Christ who are seeking to obey the
commands of Christ in the Sermon On the Mount.
When suffering for righteousness's sake the saint of
Christ must follow in the footsteps of His Master Jesus
Christ.

1 Peter 1:19-25
19 For this is thankworthy, if a
man for conscience toward
God endure grief, suffering wrongfully.

20 For what glory is it, if, when ye be buffeted for your
faults, ye shall take it patiently? but if, when ye do
well, and suffer for it, ye take it
patiently, this is acceptable with God.
21 For even hereunto were ye
called: because Christ also suffered for us, leaving us an
example, that ye should follow his steps:
22 Who did no sin, neither was guile found in his mouth:
23 Who, when he was reviled, reviled not again; when
he suffered, he threatened not; but committed
himself to him that judgeth righteously:
24 Who his own self bare our sins in his
own body on the tree, that we, being dead to
sins, should live unto righteousness: by whose stripes ye
were healed.
25 For ye were as sheep going
astray; but are now returned unto the
Shepherd and Bishop of your souls.

Notice Christs example to not exact a debut upon other
during His incarnation and walk among humanity. A
Christian looking forward to Christs rewards to His
faithful saints, must learn to walk in the way of the Lord,
to love mercy to endure grief for conscience's sake
before the Lord. Suffering wrongly at the hands of a God
hating world is normal consequence for all disciples who
openly give witness to Jesus Christ. For what difference
from among other men is there if your exact
retributions upon those who persecute you?

Or what as a disciple of Christ you are the offender. Should you not be buffeted for your actions? When you do wrong and take it patiently this is not an act of mercy. However, if you suffer wrongly being buffeted for doing right, and put retribution into the hands of God willing to suffer patiently, then you are extending mercy in the sight of God.

True Biblical mercy requires a Cross to follow in the footsteps of Jesus Christ who left us His example to follow. The Scriptures teach us our calling in the Lord, we are not to commit sins and then suffer the consequences. Instead, we are to live holy pure lives. When we are reviled for our righteous testimony of Christ, we answer not in reviling manner. No sin was found in the mouth of the Lord as they hurled curses upon Him while He hung on the Cross. What an ultimate display of love and mercy as our dear Lord took upon Himself our sins in His own body upon the Cross.

Jesus Christ threatened not, did not curse those who hated Him without cause, instead as our example of mercy committed Himself to Him who judges righteously. Even so with the disciples of Jesus Christ, when the saints entrust themselves into the hands of God seeking first the Kingdom and righteous judgment for reward. We have been forgiven by the body of Christ who His own self bare our sins in His own body upon the Cross. The suffering of the Cross, the shedding of Christs blood has by the mercy and grace of God paid for our sin debut before God. By whose wounds we are healed.

We too were like sheep being led astray by our own sin, but God had mercy, bringing us back unto the Shepherd and Bishop of our souls. Now that we have been given mercy by Gods precious gift of grace, should we not extend God's mercy to those who are not worthy too?

What is the promise for those of Christs disciples who are merciful? At the Second Coming of the Lord and at the Judgment Seat are given mercy. As all the rewards promised in the Sermon of the Mount are about Kingdom Age rewards, mercy given opens the way for the Lord to judge the merciful as qualified for the Kingdom of heaven age.

Matthew 5:8
Blessed are the pure in heart; for they shall see God.

Purity in the saints is often associated with being rewarded with seeing God. Take for example King David in the Psalms speaking of holiness which gives the worshiper access into God's presence.

Psalm 24:3-4
[3] Who shall ascend into the hill of the LORD? or who shall stand in his holy place?
[4] He that hath clean hands, and a pure heart, who hath not lifted up his soul unto vanity, nor sworn deceitfully.

The Hill of the Lord is known as Mount Zion the dwelling place of God. Access into the presence of God must accompany holiness, as seen in the incredible preparation of Old Testament Priests in Holy garments and Blood Sacrifices. King David speaks of his desire for God liken unto a priest who would ascend the Hill of the Lord where the Temple of God stood. Who could enter into the Holy presence of the Lord, those who had been sanctified by wearing Holy Garments, and washed in the blood sacrifices? This points to our personal holiness before God, as the veil which has separated God's presence and our entrance into His throne has been torn in half.

Our entrance into the Presence of God must be accompanied by personal holiness. He that has clean hands, speaking of our works before God. Also, those who have a pure heart consecrated before God. Even the result of chaste virgins in Chris who have no guile before God. Those who are given to Christ follow the Lord wherever He goes. Purity of heart gives the sanctified before the Lord the ability to stand transparent before the Lord. God has wise virgins who can enter into the Presence of God at the Marriage Supper, while the foolish virgins are shut out.
Purity of heart has given entrance to the pure of heart now, and at the coming of the Lord the right of entrance into the Kingdom of Heaven age. For the pure of heart are blessed with seeing God in ways others cannot.

Revelation 14:1-5

14 And I looked, and, lo, a Lamb stood on the mount Sion, and with him a hundred forty and four thousand, having his Father's name written in their foreheads.

² And I heard a voice from heaven, as the voice of many waters, and as the voice of a great thunder: and I heard the voice of harpers harping with their harps:

³ And they sung as it were a new song before the throne, and before the four beasts, and the elders: and no man could learn that song but the hundred and forty and four thousand, which were redeemed from the earth.

⁴ These are they which were not defiled with women; for they are virgins. These are they which follow the Lamb whithersoever he goeth. These were redeemed from among men, being the first fruits unto God and to the Lamb.

⁵ And in their mouth was found no guile: for they are without fault before the throne of God.

Notice how the Chaste Virgins are gathered unto the Lord first in harvest, as they are first fruits unto God. Consider the order of harvest when the fruits ripen in a crop. The fruit from a crop which ripens first before the others are called first fruits. These ripe fruits are taken from among the rest of the harvest which has yet to fully ripen. The first fruits are taken first into market and are highly valued as being the first of harvest. First fruits demand a higher price as they are more valuable being the first brought into the store house and into the market. So are the Chaste Virgins of Christ as we can see them taken into the Throne room before the rest of the harvest. In these ways we can see how the pure in heart have been given special access into God's presence in some ways the impure are not able to experience.

Another example of how personal purity in the life of Christs disciples gives them access into the presence of God is promised in the book of Hebrews. The Scriptures speak of rewards for the pure of heart. While Scriptures also warn God's people of the consequences of an impure heart. Notice the warning of the loss to God's people whom He refuses entrance into His promised rest at the end of the age. The Scriptures compare Israel's failure to enter their promised land, to the Christian who through an impure heart will fail to enter into the Kingdom age at the Second Coming of Jesus Christ. Many modern teachers refuse to teach from Hebrews the Scriptures which say a Christian can have an evil heart of unbelief in departing from the living God.

Hebrews 3:11-16
[11] So I sware in my wrath, They shall not enter into my rest.
[12] Take heed, brethren, lest there be in any of you an evil heart of unbelief, in departing from the living God.
[13] But exhort one another daily, while it is called To day; lest any of you be hardened through the deceitfulness of sin.

14 For we are made partakers of Christ if we hold the beginning of our confidence stedfast unto the end.
15 While it is said, Today if ye will hear his voice, harden not your hearts, as in the provocation.
16 For some, when they had heard, did provoke: howbeit not all that came out of Egypt by Moses.

Can A Christian Have An Evil Heart

Today many Scriptures are ignored or overlooked which describe the difficulty of the Christian faith. A superficial type of Christianity appeals to the masses which has eliminated the Cross, and deeper levels of commitment to Jesus Christ. If there is an issue today in a Christian's life, it is based upon the struggle with sin, the flesh, the world, and evil spirits. Simply put the flesh is more prevalent in the lives of Christians than we would like to admit. However, can we even go further into our walk of faith, and confront some aspects of Christian behavior as evil, or even Christians having an evil heart?

Instead of a subjective opinion, or an emotional response the Scriptures themselves give us the correct answer. Hebrews chapter 3 describes how Christians can have an evil heart in unbelief similar to what happened to Israel in the wilderness.
Hebrews 3:12-13
12 Take heed, brethren, lest there be in any of you an evil heart of unbelief, in departing from the living God.

13 But exhort one another daily, while it is called To day; lest any of you be hardened through the deceitfulness of sin.

The breakdown of the Scripture warns "brethren," not unbelievers of the practice of sin, which leads to a hardening of the heart, and a departure from God. Israel in the wilderness, tempted the Lord ten times with sins and practices of unbelief. The final temptation was to deny the Lord would give them the promised Land, and they refused to enter into the promised inheritance. With this generation the Lord was not pleased, and their bodies fell in the wilderness outside of God's promise of inheritance.

The Scriptures says to exhort one another daily, as the temptation to depart from the Lord by sinful practices is very real. Even today we see in the Church a very casual attitude about sin, and many Christians live for the world, or even openly live-in sin. At what cost though? They will not partake of Christ at the end of this age. What does that mean?

Just like when sinful Israel refused to follow the Lord, rebelling in sin, God promised with an oath they would not enter the promised land. (the inheritance) Now we have a promise of rest at the end of the age, the millennial kingdom which is given as an inheritance to us. However, the Sculptures warn Christians which depart from the Lord in this present evil age, will "not

inherit the Kingdom of heaven." These saints have an evil heart of unbelief in departing from the living God and will be shut out from the inheritance at the Second Coming of Jesus Christ. They will not be partakers of Christ in celebrating the inheritance being refused entrance, as Jesus Christ will say; "depart from Me you workers of iniquity, for I never knew you."
(Matthew 7:22-23)

God gave an "oath of exclusion," by which sinful Israel could not enter the promised land at the end of their journey. They had tempted the Lord by their sin and unbelief, and in Judgment God shut them out and their bodies fell in the wilderness outside of their inheritance.

Let us then serve the Lord with fear and reverence, as not everyone who says Lord, Lord, shall enter the Kingdom of Heaven. The reason being these saints hardened their hearts to God by the deceitfulness of sinful practices, and at the Judgment Seat of Christ will be refused entrance into their inheritance.

Hebrews 4:1
1 Let us therefore fear, lest a promise being left us of entering into his rest, any of you should seem to come short of it.

Hebrews 12:14-17
14 Follow peace with all men, and holiness, without which no man shall see the Lord:

15 Looking diligently lest any man fail of the grace of God; lest any root of bitterness springing up trouble you, and thereby many be defiled.
16 Lest there be any fornicator, or profane person, as Esau, who for one morsel of meat sold his birthright.
17 For ye know how that afterward, when he would have inherited the blessing, he was rejected: for he found no place of repentance, though he sought it carefully with tears.

Esau An Example of An Apostate Christians

By its very nature apostasy can only be committed by a person after first coming into saving faith, then denying the faith. The sin of apostasy can only be committed by born again Christians. This might be confusing to some who always teach the Lord keeps those He saves. However, the sin of apostasy is committed willfully against the Spirit of Grace.

Hebrews 10:29
Of how much sorer punishment, suppose ye, shall he be thought worthy, who hath trodden underfoot the Son of God, and hath counted the blood of the covenant, wherewith he was sanctified, an unholy thing, and hath done despite unto the Spirit of grace?

Notice what are the conditions involved in committing the sin of apostasy. You trample underfoot the Son of God when you openly deny Christ after being born again. An apostate Christian makes a willful decision to count the Blood of Jesus Christ, wherein he has been forgiven, and given eternal life, of no value. All this betrayal of the Lord is done against the Holy Spirit, who has given grace to the saints for every situation in life.

Now Esau is set forth in the Book of Hebrews as a man who despised the inheritance, the right of Gods covenantal blessing, and sold his birth right for the "carnal pleasures" of sin for a season. Esau was the first-born son, the legal heir to his father's kingdom, but sold his birth right making little of the future inheritance. When the time of the transfer of the kingdom came Esau, was rejected though he sought it with tears. The right of the first born was given to Jacob, who highly valued his father's inheritance. Jacob wrestled with both God and man for the right of the first-born son.

Now many modern-day Christians have wrongly assumed you can be a friend of the world, and still be a friend with God. Instead, the world has gained their affections and desires, and in a thousand ways over time, you sell out your devotion to Jesus Christ. A million times over You compromise with the world until the value of Christ is made nothing. Like Esau, You has sold out your rights to a future kingdom rule, "you shall not inherit the kingdom of heaven."

What does this mean? Were they never saved in the first place? Absolutely not, they are blood washed born again sons who never went through the process of discipline and maturation. They lived for sin, and maybe the sin of the grosser kind, as Esau was a fornicator. They are sons by birth, but illegitimate sons who never submitted to the correction and discipline of their Father. Their loss is at the Judgment Seat of Christ where they will be disqualified and shall not inherit the Kingdom of Heaven.

Does this mean they lose their salvation? The answer; once a Son always a Son by birth. They lose the right of the first-born Son, the right of inheritance. The right to their Fathers business and kingdom. They lose the right of being a King Priest in the next age where they would have ruled with Christ in the Millennial Kingdom. For Jesus Christ said, not everyone who says to Me Lord Lord shall enter the Kingdom of Heaven, but only they who do the will of My Father. Their sonship is retained, but like Esau they are disinherited from their Fathers kingdom. Apostate Christians are disinherited Christians who sold their birth right for the pleasures of sin and the love of this world.

At the Judgment Seat of Christ Apostate Christians fall into to the hands of a living God, where vengeance is executed by God against his own sons. In this case vengeance is a form of rejection and discipline, not an abandonment of sons into Hell. Instead, a disqualification, a losing of the crown, and the loss of the prize of the high calling. As the apostle Paul warmed

Christians who practice the works of the flesh, " you shall not inherit the Kingdom of God." (Galatians 5:21)

For we must all appear before the Judgment Seat of Christ to give an account for things done in the body. Things done both good and bad. Therefore, knowing the terror of the Lord, we persuade men...

Hebrew 10:26-36
26 For if we sin willfully after that we have received the knowledge of the truth, there remaineth no more sacrifice for sins,
27 But a certain fearful looking for of judgment and fiery indignation, which shall devour the adversaries.
28 He that despised Moses' law died without mercy under two or three witnesses:
29 Of how much sorer punishment, suppose ye, shall he be thought worthy, who hath trodden underfoot the Son of God, and hath counted the blood of the covenant, wherewith he was sanctified, an unholy thing, and hath done despite unto the Spirit of grace?
30 For we know him that hath said, Vengeance belongeth unto me, I will recompense, saith the Lord. And again, The Lord shall judge his people. 1 It is a fearful thing to fall into the hands of the living God.
32 But call to remembrance the former days, in which, after ye were illuminated, ye endured a great fight of afflictions.

33 Partly, whilst ye were made a gazingstock both by reproaches and afflictions; and partly, whilst ye became companions of them that were so used.

34 For ye had compassion of me in my bonds, and took joyfully the spoiling of your goods, knowing in yourselves that ye have in heaven a better and an enduring substance.

35 Cast not away therefore your confidence, which hath great recompence of reward.

36 For ye have need of patience, that, after ye have done the will of God, ye might receive the promise.

Matthew 5:9
Blessed are the peacemakers: for they shall be called the children of God.

Blessed Are the Peacemakers

The Sermon On the Mount is a mini version of the Christian walk of faith. With today's world unrest a Christian must keep their heart, as lawlessness will increase and abound. Jesus Christ taught the commands of the Sermon On the Mount for disciples to walk in a righteousness contrary to the ways of the world. Are you as a Christian getting all caught up in the politics of our day? Behind the anger and hate are the evil malevolent spirits which are stirring up the unrest, hate, and anger. One thing is for certain as the days grow shorter in relationship to the Second Coming everything which can be shaken will be shaken. The stability which once occupied the United States is being removed and darkness is growing more intense. As man will not have peace and is pushed by the evil of the day, the sons of God must keep their peace in the Lord. All manner of wars are predicted for the last days as Kingdom rises against Kingdom, and nations against nation, tribes, tongues, and families will be at odds. A nation divided within itself cannot stand; a family divided will be the course of the last days. The Sons of God must find their place in the midst of intensifying evil as peace makers.

Blessed are the peace makers for they shall be called the children of God. Peace is a true characteristic of the indwelling Holy Spirit. For we have not been given a spirit of fear, for peace will be taken from the earth as the antichrist spirit drives men mad with fear. A true division is manifesting, a separation of the righteous and the wicked. Are you mad and angry over all the injustice? Will you have anger and the works of the flesh? Of course, Christians must stand up for what is right, but in the fruit of the Spirit. You must not give to the flesh and must not lose your peace. For the anger of man does not achieve the righteousness of God. As justice is taken from the earth anger and hate will be the course of the day. Those who see the wickedness must draw near to the Lord finding God's peace in the midst of all the turmoil. True Christian faith will be marked by supernatural peace which God gives His disciples in the midst of great turmoil.

The peace makers will have kept their minds stayed upon the Lord who will keep them in perfect peace. These are the children of God at rest in the good fight of faith. For all the anger and hate is designed to keep men at war, and away from seeking God. As darkness grows so must God's children find peace. The world is being tormented with evil, Satan is releasing all manner of evil spirits to torment humanity. Even Christians are targets, tormenting evil spirits attacking God's children without mercy. You find your refuge in the Lord as you drawn near to God resisting Satan, he must flee. These will be the days of being hidden in Christ, knowing the place of refuge the secret place of prayer. An intimate knowledge of the blood of Jesus Christ for the forgiveness of sin. No grounds of accusation by evil spirits because of unconfessed sin in your life. Also, a knowledge of the authority given to the believer in the name of Jesus. The ability to wrestle with evil spirits who are attacking you using prayer and the name of Jesus to resist the devil.

Peace is the saint's portion. Gods' children are marked by a different Spirit. The absence of fear, and the peace of God which rules our hearts and minds. Do you have peace with God, and with yourself? Are you letting Satan steal your peace? Are you fearful, anxious, full of worry, and sad and depressed? Are you being oppressed by an unseen enemy who wants you to be in torment? It is time to get your eyes off all the circumstances, all the voices, all the feelings, and find rest in Jesus Christ. Peace is your promise in Christ even in the midst of impossible circumstances. God will never leave you or forsake you. As you walk through the flood, the waters which threaten to drown you, God will have to part the waters making a way through. When you walk through the fiery trials do not be surprised that such evil has come to test you. God will stand with you in the midst of the fire, and you will come forth from the fiery furnace which was prepared to your destruction. How can you make it? Gods' peace will keep you. Do not be afraid. It is a sign to your enemies of their certain destruction, but for you of your salvation.

Isaiah 43:1-2
1 But now thus saith the Lord that created thee, O Jacob, and he that formed thee, O Israel, Fear not: for I have redeemed thee, I have called thee by thy name; thou art mine.
2 When thou passes through the waters, I will be with thee; and through the rivers, they shall not overflow thee: when thou walkest through the fire, thou shalt not be burned; neither shall the flame kindle upon thee.

John 14:25-31
25 These things have I spoken unto you, being yet present with you.
26 But the Comforter, which is the Holy Ghost, whom the Father will

send in my name, he shall teach you all
things, and bring all things to
your remembrance, whatsoever I have said unto you.
27 Peace I leave with you, my peace I give unto
you: not as the world giveth, give I unto you. Let not
your heart be troubled, neither let it be afraid.
28 Ye have heard how I said unto you, I go
away, and come again unto you. If ye loved me, ye
would rejoice, because I said, I go unto the
Father: for my Father is greater than I.
29 And now I have told you before it come to
pass, that, when it is come to pass, ye might believe.
30 Hereafter I will not talk much with you: for the
prince of this world cometh, and hath nothing in me.
31 But that the world may know that I love the
Father; and as the Father gave me commandment, even
so I do. Arise, let us go hence.

Chapter Two
Persecuted For Righteousness
Matthew 5:10
Blessed are they who have been persecuted for
righteous sake; for theirs is the Kingdom of Heaven.

Blessed Are You When You Are Persecuted For
Righteousness Sake

Persecution was to be a big part of authentic disciples'
life. The first century Church experienced terrific hated
from the Roman Empire, and even at the hands of their

own countrymen. Early Christians were put into lions and gladiator arenas, others were crucified, beheaded, or made to be human torches. Rome was a demonic kingdom, and the Caesars of Rome were cruel tyrants against the first century Church.

Jesus Christ knew how the Pharisees would rise to deliver Him to Rome for crucifixion. Also knew the original disciples would pay with their lives in service to Jesus Christ. In preparation for the suffering true disciples of Jesus Christ were expected to endure, Christ spoke of the blessings which would come by being faithful in the midst of suffering for righteousness's sake. The promise from the Lord in the Sermon On the Mount is for those who endure persecution for righteousness's sake, are to be rewarded in the next age by qualifying for ruling and reigning with Jesus Christ in the Kingdom of Heaven Age.

The Break down in the Sermon On the Mount relating to persecution is completely contrary to the world's beliefs.

Matthew 5:10-16

10 Blessed are they which are persecuted for righteousness' sake: for theirs is the kingdom of heaven.

Connected to the other Beatitudes is the Lords blessing upon His disciples who are persecuted for living right for the Lord. A big part of the persecution is the result of Christs disciples teaching the commands and doctrines of Christ. Also, the command of the Lord to make disciples of all nations by preaching the Gospel all of creation.

11 Blessed are ye, when men shall
revile you, and persecute you, and shall say all manner of evil against you falsely, for my sake.

As the Gospel of Salvation goes forth and calls men to repentance by faith in Jesus Christ. The problem lies with mankind's love of darkness and hated of the light. The reason fallen mankind will not come to the light is the unwillingness to have their evil deeds exposed. Instead, men will rise up to attack the Lords messengers, and the Lord pronounces a blessing when men shall revile you. When men rise up in all manner of evil to speak out against you falsely. Just like what men did as false witnesses against Jesus Christ condemning Him unto death.

12 Rejoice, and be exceeding
glad: for great is your reward in heaven: for so persecut ed they the prophets which were before you.

The suffering comes from giving witness to Jesus Christ and living openly for Jesus Christ. Suffering now in this age as a disciple of Jesus Christ leads to loss now or even, martyrdom. As the saints are persecuted Christ gives great promise. Rejoice and be exceedingly glad for great is your reward in heaven. For all who live Godly will suffering persecution, but Christ's promise is great reward in the next age. The disciples who suffer injustice because of love for Jesus Christ are compared to the prophets of the Old Testament who had to stand up to apostate Israel in their day. Entrance into the Kingdom age is based upon suffering for Christ in this age. Notice how the apostle Paul confirms Jesus' message in the Sermon On the Mount. It is a token of Gods righteous judgment when the saints are persecuted for righteousness. Paul affirms the saints are counted worthy for the coming Kingdom age for which they suffer.

2 Thessalonians 1:3-5

3 We are bound to
thank God always for you, brethren, as it
is meet, because that your faith growth, and the
charity of every one of you all toward each
other aboundeth;
4 So that we ourselves glory in you in the churches of
God for your patience and faith in all yourpersecutions a
nd tribulations that ye endure:
5 Which is a manifest token of the
righteous judgment of God, that ye may be counted
worthy of the kingdom of God, for which ye also suffer:

Why does Christ allow for the saints to suffer in this age? The Church of Jesus Christ was meant to be a preserving agent against the corruption of a fallen world. The Lord teaches His disciples men born of the Holy Spirit are the salt of the earth. However, his admonition comes with warning if salt has lost its saltiness, it is good for nothing but to be cast out and trodden under foot of men. The warning comes with a time when the Church will commit a Great Apostasy at the end of the age. A perilous time when Christians will depart from the faith giving heed to seducing spirits and doctrines of demons.

Matthew 5:13

13 Ye are the salt of the earth: but if the salt have lost his savour, wherewith shall it be salted? is thenceforth good for nothing, but to be cast out, and to be trodden under foot of men.

Another aspect to Disciples of Jesus Christ suffering as a witness of Jesus Christ, is the saints are the light of the world. Called out from every nation of the earth and joined unto the Lord Jesus Christ, a city set upon a hill. The light of the saints and the city comes from the Lord who in the truest sense is the Light of the World. The light of Christ shines into the darkness and men cannot overpower it. The witness of Christ is not to be downplayed or hidden, instead it is to stand out in stark contrast to the world. Each believer is to carry the light

of Christ out into the world. Christians are not to put a
veil over the light instead set it up like a candlestick so it
may illumine the house so all may see.

Matthew 5:14-15

14 Ye are the light of the world. A city that is set on an
hill cannot be hid.
15 Neither do men light a candle, and put it under a
bushel, but on a candlestick; and light unto that
are in the house.

So here is the command of the Lord Jesus Christ with His
disciples knowing they will suffer for their faith. Let your
light shine before men, so they may see your works of
righteousness. The Scriptures speak of good works
which lead to future kingdom age rewards, even though
now for a season the saints must face fiery trials. As
men see the faithfulness of the saints in good works,
and endurance under persecution they are witnessed to
works which glorifies our Father which is in heaven.

16 Let your light so shine before men, that they may
see your good works, and glorify your Father
which in heaven.

The Light and Salt

When Jesus Christ preached the Sermon On the Mount,
He gave the character of those who would qualify as His
disciples. So contrary to the ways of the world are the

characteristics of the Kingdom, anyone who would live by them would become the light and salt of the earth. Why is this so? The world is considered in a dark fallen state, its main characteristic is corruption from sin and death. As long as man is still in his mortal state, we must understand corruption is reigning through sin. The kingdom of darkness as ruled by its chief Prince of the Power of the Air, Satan, lords it over fallen man. Satan stands as the over lord with every man who by nature of corruption is a son of Gods wrath. So contrary to God is fallen man are by nature are hateful to God and love the darkness because of their love of sin. The world we grow up in and consider as normal life loves darkness and hates the light and will not come to the light to have their evil deeds exposed. When a man repents and turns to faith in Christ he is delivered from an evil corrupt nature and has a new nature which has the love of Jesus Christ. The born-again child of God is delivered from the Kingdom of Darkness and is placed in the Kingdom of the Dear Son Jesus Christ.

A man born of Christ's Spirit is no longer in the darkness and has become a child of the light. The governing principles of Christ's life indwelling a man born again leads them to live after what to contrary to the rest of this present evil age. Such a man will feel alien to the rest of the world, separated from the world on a pilgrimage towards the Second Coming, in the world but not of it. A life so contrary to the worlds system it is a natural reproof to men who love darkness. In reality such a disciple of Jesus Christ has become the light and salt of the earth.

Will the organization of Church then save the entire world? As the true Church is comprised of born-again sons and daughters, can Church organization make for a Christian world? The answer comes from Jesus Christ, a warning which states the Church can lose its salt and be cast out trodden underfoot by man. Have you seen the danger which comes from the corruptive nature of the world, and the Church conforming to the world? When the Church looks more like the world, acts more like the world, talks more like the world it has fallen and is no longer a true witness of Jesus Christ. It has lost its Christ like character has fallen into darkness and is being trampled underfoot by man.

Will the Church take over the world, or be trampled under in the state of apostasy? Right now, we have greedy leaders who want to profit off the Church. Multimillionaires who build huge mansions, who drive the best cars who live Luxurious lives. Others who live immoral lives are self-entitled and take to satisfy their lustful cravings. A carnal Church lead by evil imposters is waxing worse and worse, men and women who are more concerned about seeking wealth, and popularity than God. Whose belly is their God, who have given themselves over to play acting the Christian life. Who preach a false Gospel of wealth and riches, and worldwide conquest by the Church? Who with great swelling words of promise boast of the Churches power and conquest? However, the Church lies in ruins, glorious in the eyes of man, in the eyes of God poor, blind, miserable, and naked.

Do the leaders of modern organized Church demonstrate the characteristics of the Sermon On the Mount? Here are some warning passages from the Sermon On the Mount which teach Christians will be held accountable according to the commands given by Christ in the Sermon.
The warnings are against any man who teaches against these commands, or who will not keep these commands. Any person in or outside of the Church who is judged for such disobedience will be called the least by God as He qualifies the saints for the Kingdom of Heaven age. In the same judgment any man who will keep the commands of the Sermon On the Mount, and who will teach them shall be called great in the Kingdom of Heaven age.

Now comes the warning of Kingdom exclusion for all Christians who display hypocrisy in serving the Lord. Any man who pretends submission to the Lord but breaks the commandments of the Lord will be disinherited at the Judgment Seat of Christ. For except your righteousness exceeds the righteousness of the Scribes and Pharisees, you (any Christian) shall in no case enter the Kingdom of Heaven. How great is this warning which often is overlooked by a hyper grace mentality? For the righteousness which is measured is the righteous acts of faith after one has been saved by the righteousness of God in Christ. Your works are measured not the free gift of eternal life.

Matthew 5:19-20
19 Whosoever therefore shall break one of these least commandments, and shall teach men so, he shall be called the least in the kingdom of heaven: but whosoever shall do and teach them, the same shall be called great in the kingdom of heaven. 20 For I say unto you, That except your righteousness shall exceed the righteousness of the scribes and Pharisees, ye shall in no case enter into the kingdom of heaven.

What is the problem with the Pharisees? "But woe unto you scribes and Pharisees. Hypocrites. For you shut up the Kingdom of heaven against men: for you neither go in yourselves, neither suffer you them that are entering to go in" Religious pretenders are the peril of the day as they reject the Lordship of Jesus Christ and teach against His commandments. What the religious hypocrite does is to be seen of man. In doing so they are glorified by man and exploit the Church for personal gain and profit. They will devour widows' houses exploiting the week, and then put on a show making for long prayers so men will think them spiritual. They stop men from finding the narrow way which leads to the Kingdom and bring men under their bondage.

Hypocrites make disciples after their image and kingdom, who disciples become even more hypocritical children of Hell.

Matthew 23:13-15
13 But woe unto
you, scribes and Pharisees, hypocrites! for ye shut up the kingdom of heaven
against men: for ye neither go
in yourselves, neither suffer ye them that are entering to go in.
14 Woe unto
you, scribes and Pharisees, hypocrites! for ye devour widows' houses, and for a
pretense make long prayer: therefore ye shall receive the greater damnation.
15 Woe unto
you, scribes and Pharisees, hypocrites! for ye compass sea and land to make one
proselyte, and when he is made, ye make him twofold more the child of hell than yourselves.

As we continue to examine the commands of the Sermon On the Mount, we will see the vast difference between the disciples of Jesus Christ, and the hypocrisy of religious hypocrites. The Lord teaches how to pray in secret, to be openly rewarded by the Lord at the Second Coming. While the religious hypocrites do everything to be seen of men whose reward is the praise of men. In this way religious hypocrites compromise the commands of the Lord, and forfeit Kingdom age rewards for the praise of man now.

The same thing could be said in those who seek the Kingdom or put wealth and riches before the Lord. Religious hypocrites often hide their true motives in wanting to exploit the Church for personal gain and riches. Today we have self-proclaimed apostles and prophets who have become multi-millionaires by profiting off the Church. They profess their ministries are the way of the Kingdom of Heaven on earth, rejecting the teaching of Kingdom future at the Second Coming of Jesus Christ. In reality drawn disciples away from the Lord and unto themselves. Their religious hypocrisy will be judged at the Judgement Seat of Christ where all the wood, hay, and stubble of their Kingdom building will burn up in the judicial fires of Christ.

The Lord warns they have their reward now and will be shut out from Kingdom of heaven entrance. " You shall in no case enter the Kingdom of Heaven." Which is a big topic of the Sermon On the Mount which has been grossly misunderstood by modern Church doctrine. As Jesus disqualifies religious hypocrites from Kingdom of heaven entrance at the end of this age. Many Christians have reasoned those men were never saved in the first place. Or a Second way is to say those who were shut up from the Kingdom were truly Christian but lost their salvation. Instead of either of those two beliefs, let us consider Kingdom Exclusion by Christians not qualifying at the Judgment Seat. What does this actually mean? As we continue to break down the message of the Sermon On the Mount issues about the coming Kingdom age will be become abundantly clear.

Loss of Kingdom or Loss of Eternal Life

I have changed my position over the last several years from one who could lose his salvation to one who cannot. I have come out of the prophetic Charismatic Movement where just about everything is centered in man. So, learning to keep doctrines in the centrality of Jesus Christ has helped me see other positions, and their Scriptural integrity. Having held the former position of losing eternal life at the Judgment Seat of Christ no longer seems viable to me according to Scriptures. However, there are ample warnings of being shut out or excluded when Jesus Christ returns. It appears judgment upon Christians is very real, and failure results in some manner of loss or punishment. If you are a typical Calvinist, you explain away judgment passages by hitting the default button of Calvin theology and say they were never saved to begin with. The doctrine of the Perseverance of the saints has no place for Christian failure in Calvinism. However, I do agree with Calvinists that once a man, woman, or child has received eternal life from faith in Jesus Christ they can never lose eternal life. So, in this way they are saved from eternal damnation in the Lake of Fire which is the final judgment.

Now Armenian Theologians recognize judgment upon failed Christians at the Judgment Seat of Christ. They do not go beyond Scriptures as the Calvinist teach stating they were never saved in the first place. However, they do go beyond what the Scriptures teach in judgment stating Christians can die in their sins and go to Hell, and eternal damnation in the Lake of Fire. In effect Armenian Theology teaches the loss of salvation and eternal life even after a man has been born again. One must challenge the legitimacy of sending a born-again child of God to Hell even if they have committed gross sins. I know there are warnings in the Scriptures of an unpardonable sin in which there is no repentance or forgiveness. I would consider the sin of Ananias and Sapphira in acts chapter five, and their sudden deaths as an example of the unpardonable sin. You must then decide by the volume of Scriptures did Ananias and Sapphira lose their salvation and go to Hell?

Its apparent Christians are judged at the Second Coming of Jesus Christ. However, the loss is of kingdom age rewards and entrance. Once one is truly born again with a new creation nature, their sins have been forgiven by the substitutionary sacrifice of Jesus Christ. The end result is redemption in His blood by a perfect sacrifice which can never pass away or fail. The Cross has given those born of the Holy Spirit eternal redemption and eternal life. However, the Cross does not automatically qualify Christs disciples for entrance into the Kingdom of Heaven. The Sermon On the Mount is one of the Scriptural evidence of Kingdom exclusion.

Kingdom Confusion

Contrary to popular Kingdom of Heaven Theology a lot of confusion has come concerning what the Kingdom of Heaven really is. First in the Lord's Prayer, why should Christians pray for the Kingdom to come, "if it is already here." Why pray for the will of the Lord to be done if it already is happening? Did you notice the Kingdom has predated the formation of the Church, as it was prepared before the foundation of the world? When Jesus Christ announced the Kingdom of Heaven was at hand, it is the same as saying the Kingdom is near. Why not just say the "kingdom of heaven is here?" When the Pharisees demanded to know when the Kingdom would come, Jesus Christ said it would come without observation. Even upon the Resurrection of Jesus Christ, the original disciples asked Jesus, "will you at this time restore the Kingdom to Israel."(Acts 1:6) All the disciples we are still looking for the Kingdom in their day, which means it had yet to come.

What is the problem? The modern Church has made the Kingdom of Heaven to mean the Church, and the glory of God spread through the Church all over the world. There are so many problems making the Kingdom the Church, the first being the almost 2000 years of Church corruption. The Kingdom of Heaven is the will of God done on earth. Jesus Christ warned not everyone who says to Me Lord Lord will enter the Kingdom of Heaven, but they which do the will of My Father. Let us get Real Church history demonstrates incredible bloodshed by the Holy Wars, and Inquisitions. The Kingdom of Heaven never has been the Catholic Church, or the Pope as it is King.

Next, why would the Scriptures warn Christians can be disqualified from the Kingdom? The Kingdom is to be entered into at the Second Coming of Jesus Christ, some will be shut out. How can the Kingdom be entered into now, and then again at the Second Coming? The Kingdom is also connected to Abraham, Isaac, and Jacob, which would require their resurrection to be a part. The Parables of Talents, Pounds, and 10 Virgins teach Kingdom Age rewards are not given until the Second Coming. Jesus Christ told His apostles they would be given the Kingdom when the Lord would be given the throne of His glory, and the apostles would become immortal, and given 12 thrones to rule with Him.

Let us get real, the Scriptures teach the Kingdom of Heaven is future, at the Second Coming, when the Lord brings the Kingdom with Him. Entrance into the Kingdom requires the resurrection of the righteous dead, an immortal body of the saints. When Jesus Christ sits on the Throne of David ruling from the New Jerusalem as the King of the earth. Is at the time of the

Second Coming the Kingdoms of this world become the Kingdom of our Lord and His Christ. The Kingdom of Heaven is to be entered into at the return of Jesus Christ, not all who say Lord, Lord will be quaffed to enter, even though they are born again of the Holy Spirit. Which proves being saved by grace, does not guarantee Kingdom of Heaven entrance by all Christians. This is why modern-day Kingdom Now Theology cannot answer the Scriptures which speak of Kingdom disqualification, or Kingdom Exclusion disqualifying many Christians.

The Kingdom of Heaven is not given at the new birth, the born-again experience. The Kingdom of Heaven is represented as Christ's.
 inheritance given upon qualifications at the Judgment Seat of Christ. The Cross of Jesus Christ gives us eternal life, while works of righteousness done after coming into saving faith are what qualifies or disqualifies born again Christians from Kingdom entrance. Christians who are disqualified from entering the Kingdom, are not sent to Hell. Instead, they have lost their inheritance even though they still maintain their position of a born-again son of God. This is why Paul warns Christians who continue in the works of the flesh "will not inherit the Kingdom of God." So, the Kingdom of Heaven first proclaimed by Jesus Christ is not yet present and must be qualified, at the end of the present age, the Second Coming, and Jesus Christ physically present as King over all the earth.

To make the Kingdom a spiritual birth in our hearts is inaccurate. Yes, we are born again, and placed in the Kingdom of the dear Son, with whom we have redemption in His blood. The sovereign rule of God is a big part of our lives, His rule as God is certain. However, the Kingdom of Heaven is very specific, the rule of Christ on earth with His glorified saints, like Abraham, Isaac, and Jacob. So, the Kingdom of Heaven cannot be a spiritual kingdom in our hearts, the sovereign rule of God now, or already entered and given to Christians. Instead, it is future at the Second Coming, and the resurrection of the righteous dead into immortality. Where some Christians will be disqualified and will not enter the Kingdom of Heaven age.

Matthew 8:10-12
10 When Jesus heard it, he marveled, and said to them that followed, Verily I say unto you, I have not found so great faith, no, not in Israel.
11 And I say unto you, That many shall come from the east and west, and shall sit down with Abraham, and Isaac, and Jacob, in the kingdom of heaven.
12 But the children of the kingdom shall be cast out into outer darkness: there shall be weeping and gnashing of teeth.

Matthew 19:23-30
23 Then said Jesus unto his disciples, Verily I say unto you, That a rich man shall hardly enter into the kingdom of heaven.

24 And again I say unto you, It is easier for a camel to go through the eye of a needle, than for a rich man to enter into the kingdom of God.

25 When his disciples heard it, they were exceedingly amazed, saying, Who then can be saved?

26 But Jesus beheld them, and said unto them, With men this is impossible; but with God all things are possible.

27 Then answered Peter and said unto him, Behold, we have forsaken all, and followed thee; what shall we have, therefore?

28 And Jesus said unto them, Verily I say unto you, That ye which have followed me, in the regeneration when the Son of man shall sit in the throne of his glory, ye also shall sit upon twelve thrones, judging the twelve tribes of Israel.

29 And everyone that hath forsaken houses, or brethren, or sisters, or father, or mother, or wife, or children, or lands, for my name's sake, shall receive a hundredfold, and shall inherit everlasting life.

30 But many that are first shall be last; and the last shall be first.

Galatians 5:19-21

19 Now the works of the flesh are manifest, which are these, Adultery, fornication, uncleanness, lasciviousness,

20 Idolatry, witchcraft, hatred, variance, emulations, wrath, strife, seditions, heresies,

21 Envyings, murders, drunkenness, revellings, and such like: of the which I tell you before, as I have also told you in time past, that they which do such things shall not inherit the kingdom of God.

Matthew 25:31-34
31 When the Son of man shall come in his glory, and all the holy angels with him, then shall he sit upon the throne of his glory:
32 And before him shall be gathered all nations: and he shall separate them one from another, as a shepherd divideth his sheep from the goats:
33 And he shall set the sheep on his right hand, but the goats on the left.
34 Then shall the King say unto them on his right hand, Come, ye blessed of my Father, inherit the kingdom prepared for you from the foundation of the world:

Chapter Three
Warnings of Losing the Kingdom

Matthew 5:21-23

21 Ye have heard that it was said by them of old time, Thou shalt not kill; and whosoever shall kill shall be in danger of the judgment:
22 But I say unto you, That whosoever is angry with his brother without a cause shall be in danger of the judgment: and whosoever shall say to his brother, Raca, shall be in danger of the

council: but whosoever shall say, Thou fool, shall be in danger of hell fire.

Brotherly Love
As the Church moving towards the Second Coming of Jesus Christ the saints must watch out not to fall into cold love. As lawlessness abounds the love of many will grow cold. The Church as we have known it in America has changed, the commercialism is causing the Church to fall to the ground as the man-made system is dying out. What remains are those who have been truly born of the Holy Spirit who have a new creation nature in Christ. All those born of the Spirit are included in the body of Christ and are unified by having the same indwelling of the Holy Spirit. With a changed nature we love the Lord keeping the first commandment, while loving our brothers in Christ is our proof of loving the Lord. How can we say we love the Lord whom we cannot see, while not loving our brother in Christ whom we can see?

It is time for those born of the Holy Spirit to clearly see the battle over brotherly love. We cannot follow the worlds system and love the Lord or give ourselves to love the brethren. The end times battle is coming down to the most ancient of battles, Cain, and Abel. The Spirit of Antichrist is preparing the world to accept the False Messiah and is attacking the true Church. The division we see amongst Christians is in the lack of discernment in exposing the Spirit of Antichrist in our midst. The saints must come to understand false doctrines abound which divides the Church into factions and divisions called sects. How is it you love the brothers of your sect, those who follow the same apostle or prophet, but you are cold to those outside your organization? The division is artificial, as the body of Christ is divided by those we lift up into unnatural positions over our lives. I cannot afford to divide from my brother in Christ along any sectarian ground. As no doctrine in Christ commands me to do so, or no leader in the Church can lead me to hate or reject my brother in the Lord.

I cannot put politics before the Lord or reject my brother over political differences. As the battle between Cain and Abel will come down to the love of the world, or the saint's separation from it. For all the world has to offer is summoned up in the lust of the flesh, luster of the eyes and the pride of life. Loving the world is not consistent with the Christian faith as it forces me to choose against the commands of Christ. I will put something or someone before the Lord in love of the world and will end up defending my love of the world. The saints are required to love not the world which allows me to fully follow the Lord and lay down my life for the brethren.

Cain offered the fruits of the world, all which comes from being man made. Abel offered the blood Sacrifice of the Lord which is contrary to the world as its origin is solely from God and not man. The blood Sacrifice of

Jesus Christ is not manufactured by the world, so can overcome sin, and the worlds domination. How free is the man who trusts in Christ alone, and draws His life from the Lord and not the world? Sadly, the Church has fallen into talking like the world, and trying to save the world by human wisdom. The end times battle will be brother against brother and those who are playing God by attempting to save the world, and those who trust Christ alone for their salvation. Men will fight to build their kingdoms and improve the world as the mystery which comes from Babylon drives religion all over the world. Those in Christ have no kingdom to build and can see the world for its intense evil will look for salvation in Jesus Christ alone. Only God can Himself save the world and bring the Kingdom of Heaven to earth.

Cain will fight to preserve his kingdom. Abel will not hate and fight his brother as the true saint in Christ is a pilgrim on a journey. As the present evil age is not home for the saints of the Lord. Salvation comes by the Lord alone. Fulness of redemption will be realized at the Second Coming of Jesus Christ. Saints who love not the world are walking in loving the Lord and can freely love their brothers in Christ. A true righteousness will be demonstrated by those who love the Lord, walking in real freedom from sins dominion. Cain will hate the righteousness he sees in his brother and will seek to destroy the witnesses of his brother Abel. For this cause the final battle on earth will be the ancient war of Cain and Abel played out by the whole world. This is the reason why Jesus Christ warned His disciples the whole world would hate the true Church before the Second Coming.

Now is the time to choose whose nature you will display. Will you fight against those who love God and have forsaken the world? Will you love the Lord and love your brothers in Christ? For by this love will all men know you are Christ's disciples, by your love for one another.

Danger of Judging By Prejudice

Since America is a caught up in hate and anger concerning all the injustices this world has to offer, Christians need to be warned about judging your brother. First of all, racial inequality is born out of hate and abuse so there is no excuse for any reason to persecute any race. Also, unjust law enforcement is against the very basis of the laws which enforcers are there to protect. The color of a man, the race of their origin does not alter the law in the least bit. Instead ensures those very same protections and privileges afforded by the law abiding of any race is upheld and defended. Since many recent slayings of black men by police officers looked like more murder than execution of justice, the nation has been provoked to hate an anger over racial injustice. What then is the problem with Christians in the midst of a growing violence and hate of brother against brother? The danger is in

Christians being caught up in the judgments of hate, anger, and retribution.

What happens when you judge your brother in anger or hate? The law says if you murder you are in danger of eternal judgment as a murder. The law of Christ is higher and more demanding and difficult as it exceeds what is written in the Law.

"But I say unto you, That whosoever is angry with his brother without a cause shall be in danger of the judgment: and whosoever shall say to his brother, Raca, shall be in danger of the council: but whosoever shall say, Thou fool, shall be in danger of hell fire."(Matthew 5:22)

Why is the judgment of anger without a cause is serious offense? As a Christian you are in danger of judgment. Why do you hold onto offense against your brother for whom Christ died? Why do you gladly accept the grace and mercy afforded to you by the Cross of Jesus Christ, then deny it to your brother by holding onto anger, hate, offense and unforgiveness. Acting outside of the grace of God puts you in danger at the Judgment Seat of Christ. Many Christians will lose their future setting in glory simply on the basis of walking in anger and hate.

You are to leave your gift at the alter where offenses are being held against your brother or your brothers against you and seek to be reconciled with your brother.

In confronting sin, you can be angry but sin not. Many are the offenses of this life, racial hate and prejudice is one of the vilest leading to a great deal of bloodshed. The Church should not fall into racial hate and divide even if the world is locked into racial war. I am to hate sin and confront sin by exposing the deeds of darkness. To go further and hate my enemy is to put me at odds with the commands of Jesus Christ. As I am commanded by the Lord to love my enemies. How impossible if I allow racial hatred into my heart, I have no right as a disciple of Jesus Christ to judge men on the basis of race.

Whosoever shall say to his brother "Raca" meaning you are worthless is in danger of Gods Council. Judging any man by racial offense and punishing or abusing just because they come from a different race, or any other condition will be held in account before God. In America we have many cultural standards and bigotry by which we judge others. Not so in Christ, this is the work of fallen man and a fallen world of darkness. The value of any man is determined by all men being created in the image of God, race, education, gender, money , does not change a man's value before God. The price that Christ paid in His own blood for a man's soul is beyond the measure of any earthly comparison or treasure. You are invalidating the Cross by hating our brother for any reason.

Finally, Jesus Christ warns His disciples of the danger of Hell Fire for calling your brother; "you fool." Why is this important in a world where many men act like fools, endanger others, abuse, and violate others? Our message is the Cross by which we warn men of eternal judgment and the consequences of sin. We are to expose the works of darkness by bringing them to light, calling men into salvation and forgiveness. In this present evil age, many will oppose the message of the Cross, and even persecute the messenger, or even kill when their darkness is exposed. Ours is not to stand in retribution but to give place to the Lord's vindication. How difficult it is to keep our position before the Lord, extending mercy and grace to the vile and undeserving. Our temptation will be to vindicate ourselves by casting off the offender and judging them as unredeemable. However final judgment is left up to the Lord, so Christians have no right of final judgment. We can warn, and exhort, and condemn men's actions while maintaining a heart of redemption even if a man were judged by God unto death.

Vengeance should never be taken into our hands, as we leave room for the Lord's vengeance. Ours is pick up the Cross in the fellowship of the sufferings of Christ. Racial hatred will not be resolved in this present evil age as it is a form of brotherly hatred as primitive as the first two brothers Cain and Able. In the Church racial hatred is not even to be once named. Instead, Christians should be known by the Church of Philadelphia the Church of

brotherly love. A Church which only sees a man
according to Jesus Christ and the Cross.

Matthew 5:23-26
23 Therefore if thou bring thy gift to the altar, and there
rememberest that thy brother hath ought against thee.
24 Leave there thy gift before the altar and go thy way;
first be reconciled to thy brother, and then come and
offer thy gift.
25 Agree with thine adversary quickly, whiles thou art in
the way with him; lest at any time the adversary deliver
thee to the judge, and the judge deliver thee to the
officer, and thou be cast into prison.
26 Verily I say unto thee, Thou shalt by no means come
out thence, till thou hast paid the uttermost farthing.

Leaving Your Gift at the Altar

How important is brotherly love as emphasized by Jesus
Christ in the Sermon On the Mount. Disciples of Jesus
Christ are reminded of the Old Testament law which
requires gifts and offerings which are acts of worship
before God to be brought to the alter. Jesus Christ then
applies a principle of seeking your brother's forgiveness
even before the gift were to be offered.
The importance of forgiveness after coming into saving
faith is written in the Sermon On the Mount. Jesus
Christ gives a very clear warning to unforgiving disciples.
If you coming to the alter remember your brother in
Christ is holding an offense against you, leave you gift at

the altar. Jesus Christ was despised and rejected of men, a man acquainted with sorrows who bare our sins and carried our iniquities. Jesus paid the ultimate price so we could be forgiven, are we then to worship God but hold onto our brothers' offenses?

Leave your gift at the alter and go seek out your brother so any offenses can be put away by forgiveness. The warning comes with seeking to come to terms with you adversary who holds offense against you. Agree with you adversary quickly your brother in Christ, unless the Lord becomes your adversary at the Judgment Seat of Christ. Holding onto your brothers' offenses are to draw Christ's judgment against you.

Lest you brother asks for justice and recompense, resulting in a judgment and loss before the Judgment Seat of Christ. In this case the Judge is Christ, and the officer who executes the judgement too. The loss is one of the rights to the next age, and some will even suffer the greatest of penalty being cast into outer darkness. The truth of unforgiving brothers in Christ comes with the deepest of warnings for those who will not seek out forgiveness for their offenses. For verily you shall not come out of Christs judgment until you pay the penalty to the last cent. Disciples of Christ simply have no place to hold onto another person's offenses.

Chapter Four
Lusting After Women

Matthew 5:27-30

27 Ye have heard that it was said by them of old
time, Thou shalt not commit adultery:
28 But I say unto you, That whosoever looketh on a
woman to lust after her hath committed adultery with
her already in his heart.
29 And if thy right eye offend thee, pluck it out, and cast
 it from thee: for it is profitable for thee that
one of thy members should
perish, and not that thy whole body should be
cast into hell.
30 And if thy right hand offend thee, cut it off, and cast i
t from thee: for it is profitable for thee that one
of thy members should
perish, and not that thy whole body should be
cast into hell.

"Our Lord now appears as Teacher of His people. And
the fulfilment of the law spoken of is practical, — the
raising the requirements of duty above the law's level
He is setting up a loftier standard than was known to
the old covenant. The foundation-principle of the law is
Justice ; that of the Sermon on the Mount, is Mercy ;
John i. 17. Justice is a part of the character of God, and
Israel was to reflect it, But love is God's highest
perfection, and it is in connection with the new view of

God, that Jesus introduces His new commands. This part
of God's character the disciples of Christ are to imitate."
" He teaches us next, that the moral part of the law is
elevated by Himself : and He assures us, that an ignoring
of this, a consequent lower standard, with a practice
reaching only to the height of the old covenant, will
exclude, not from eternal life , but from His millennial
kingdom."
Sermon On the Mount Expounded; Robert Govett pg. 43
and 54.

The Cost of Adultery
Sexual immorality is exposed as a sin which leads to
Kingdom of Heaven exclusion. In this passage of the
Sermon On the Mount we can see the higher standards
given to the disciples of Christ than the laws given to
Israel by Moses. You have heard it said by them of old
time you shall not commit adultery. Which lends to the
6th and 9th commands of the 10 commandments.
Now Jesus teaches a righteousness which is a higher
demand, more related to motives of the heart. New
commands which reach beyond outward obedience's
right into the heart. Blessed and holy, for they are which
partake of the first resurrection. Blessed are the pure in
heart for they shall see God.
But I say unto you whosoever looks on a woman to lust
after her has committed adultery with her already in his
heart. In these days of pornography on display
everywhere, is this not a deep warning of temptation?
Jesus Christ raises the standard of the law of Moses into

the purity of heart. In the case the disciples of Christ are called to a greater accountability. Not seeing how close disciples can come to acting like the rest of the world, and still not commit the actual sin. Instead to remove yourself far away from any sources of temptation. The sexual sin which the Sermon On the Mount specifies is the sin of adultery. Which is sexual sin between married persons, or at least one person must be married. It is a breaking of the marriage covenant and the violation of the holiness of the marriage bed. Perhaps adultery best defines the destruction of marriage and the family. As the Lord continues to define adultery which leads to the breaking of the marriage covenant resulting in divorce.

Now comes some of the most difficult passages of judgment which Christians often put off onto those who are outside of Christ, and not disciples of Jesus Christ. Why the temptation to not apply these judgments to believers? The reason is not that difficult to understand. The judgments are so severe as to threaten the security of the disciples of Jesus Christ.

"And if thy right eye offend thee, pluck it out, and cast it from thee: for it is profitable for thee that one of thy members should perish, and not that thy whole body should be cast into hell."

What means a disciple of Jesus Christ can be cast into Hell? The actual word in the Greek for Hell is Gehenna. Where Hell is a very specific place in the underworld, the word Hades describes all the entire domain of the underworld. As Hades includes other portions of the underworld including Paradise, and Tartarus. The idea of believers suffering Gehenna implies some kind of punishment at the Second Coming of Jesus Christ. Punishment for what? Living a ungodly life after coming into saving faith. In this case not bringing lustful passions under the control of the Holy Spirit. Being led of the Spirit qualifies the saints for the Kingdom of Heaven. Where living after the flesh like living an adulterous life disqualifies a disciple in Christ for Kingdom of heaven age entrance.

Furthermore, the cost of adultery may include discipline of disciples during the Kingdom age. It has not been a popular doctrine with modern Christianity. Also has been perverted by the Catholic Church with the false doctrine of purgatory. The Catholics heresy of Purgatory teaches a man can be saved out from the underworld after death. However, the true doctrine is once a man dies comes the judgment, there are no second chances for man for salvation after death. The doctrine of discipline after death is for those saved by grace in this life before death. This makes the teachings of Jesus Christ then the true record.

Plucking out your right eye keeps the disciple of Christ from entering into loss at the Judgment Seat of Christ.

This is not the actual removal of the eye as lust can continue even with one eye. Instead, it refers to the disciple's willingness to deal with his own flesh putting to death the members of his body so he can serve the Lord wholly with the members of his body. For Jesus Christ teaches a Christian must put to death the lawless deeds of the body. For its more profitable that one of your members of the body should perish, than for the whole body cast into Gehenna.

Can a Christian be judged with Gehenna at the Second Coming of the Lord? Jesus Christ warns this is indeed possible.

Excerpt from Watchman Nee

"Another thing that we have to realize is that the person spoken of here must be a Christian, for only a Christian is clean in his body as a whole and can thus enter into life after dealing with his lust in a single member of his body. It would not be enough for the unbelievers to cut off a hand or a foot. Even if they were to cut off both hands and both feet, they would still have to go to hell. In order to enter the kingdom of the heavens, it is better for a Christian to have an incomplete body than to go into eternal fire because of incomplete dealing.

Following this, verse 9 says, "And if your eye stumbles you, pluck it out and cast it from you; it is better for you to enter into life with one eye than to have two eyes and be cast into the Gehenna of fire." This shows us that if a saved person does not deal with his lust, he will not be able to enter into life, but will go into eternal fire. The eternal fire here is the Gehenna of fire. The Bible shows us that a Christian has the possibility of suffering the Gehenna of fire. Although he can suffer the Gehenna of fire, he cannot suffer it forever. He can only suffer it during the age of the kingdom.

Matthew 18 is not the only portion of Scripture that says this. Other portions of the Bible also contain the same teaching. For example, the Sermon on the Mount in Matthew 5—7 contains clear words of the same kind. Matthew 5:21-22 says, "You have heard that it was said to the ancients, `You shall not murder, and whoever murders shall be liable to the judgment.' But I say to you that everyone who is angry with his brother shall be liable to the judgment. And whoever says to his brother, Raca, shall be liable to the judgment of the Sanhedrin; and whoever says, Moreh, shall be liable to the Gehenna of fire." At the beginning of chapter five, we read that the Lord Jesus saw the multitude. But He did not teach the multitude; rather, He taught the disciples (v. 1). The Sermon on the Mount is for the disciples. Therefore, the one who reviles others in verse 22 is a brother. He calls another brother Raca, that is, good-for-nothing, or Moreh, that is, a fool. When he calls his brother this way, he shall be liable to the Gehenna of fire. This does not refer to an unsaved person, for an unsaved person will go to hell even if he does not call anyone Moreh. Every time the Bible talks about works; it refers to one who belongs to God. If such a one does not belong to God, there is no need to mention such things. This is a saved person, a brother, but because he has reviled his brother, he is liable to the Gehenna of fire.

Collected Works of Watchman Nee, The (Set 2) Vol. 29: The Gospel of God (2),

(Chapter 10, Section 2)

Confession of Sexual Sin
One of the most predominant sins of culture, and among professors of the Christian faith is sexual sin. Can a genuine move of God then bypass the need to confess sins of the sexual nature? Our culture is saturated with images of glamorizing sexual sin, and sexually immoral lifestyles. Many famous persons of Hollywood and the entertainment industry are heavy promoters of sexual immorality, and celebrate sexual sin with their music, and images. Also, in the modern American Church it is statistically noted up to 80% of all Christian teenagers have participated in pre martial sex, as a natural course of dating relationships. Generally speaking, sexual immorality is simply not viewed as sin by a very large percentage of teens and young adults. Also statistically speaking a large percentage of young adults have chosen the immoral lifestyle by living together outside of marriage. Generally speaking, the American culture is hardened by the deceit of sexual immorality, it is constant promotion through the entertainment

industry, and media. Is likely one of the single greatest factors in the demise of the Church and nation, and yet is constantly celebrated and defined as love, and normal practice in life. Generally speaking, Americans now see themselves as sexually immoral, or sexually unclean, by all manner of sexual sins and perversions.

Are revivals and moves of God expected without the need from the deep repentance of sexual sin? How could that be, seeing sexual sin is tied to idolatry and worship of self? Even in the Old Testament sexual sin broke out with the nation of Israel after being freed by the Blood of the Lamb. As demonstrated at the foot of Mount Sinai, and the orgy with the Golden Calf. Cannot Christians see some of the vilest sins, and temptations to deny God, can be right in his presence? Sexual immorality is a powerful seduction, and its many various forms of Medusa's head which include fornication, adultery, homosexuality, incest, rape, pedophilia, prostitution, pornography, and general uncleanness in thoughts, words, and deeds. The power of sexual imagery is pushed upon the American culture daily, as Satan has taken this sin to bring great bondage to the Church, and the entire world.

What is the source of apathy and luke warmness in the modern organized Church? Is it due to the to the relationship with moral compromise so prevalent among Christians? We see modern revivalist, pastors, elders, and Church leaders at large falling into sexual sin

and immortality. What is one of the single largest
reason's men leave the ministry, the moral compromise
they find themselves in, being hardened in heart by
sexual sins. Resulting in the inability to repent leading to
divorce, and family breakup. When you see the
prophets, and revivalists exposed in lies and deception,
living sexually immoral lives, you can be sure the Church
has fallen into great darkness. All the while counterfeit
revivals are being proclaimed where no confession of
sexual sin is ever mentioned. If there ever has come
need for the most basic forms of the Christian faith, it is
the dire need for the Church to expose its own
darkness, sexual practices, and perversion, and cover
up. No member of the body of Christ would go
untouched if the Holy Spirit were to bring the great
conviction of sexual sins, our hearts would be broken by
the Church's carelessness and apathy.

Where is the fire of God today? Will a revival begin
outside the Church by immoral men, who have come
into saving faith? The passion, the zeal a new Christian
has to call men to God, and to denounce their former
lives of sin, of sexual perversion and immorality. It
seems the Holy Spirit must press upon the Church back
again into the basics of moral purity. Will it take a man
or woman who has come out of the perversion to
confront the Church? I can see no real genuine move of
God, without the confrontation of sexual immorality.
Men and women who are dramatically saved out of
those sins and lifestyles calling the Church back to God.

If mass conversions are being declared, without the confession of transformation out of sexual perversity, I doubt the move is truly from the Holy Spirit. A truly born-again man will be transformed into a holy and pure nature. Will no longer participate in the evil deeds of sexual immorality for the sake of the things the wrath of God is coming upon the sons of disobedience.

The Bible makes it clear the acts of uncleanness produced by sexual sin should not even be named once among us. Christians are not to be partakers with the immoral. Instead, we are to expose the hidden things of darkness, which are so perverse, they should not even be mentioned once among the saints. A clear move of God will bring the hidden things of darkness to light, and sex sins by the multitudes will be laid on Gods alter in true confession and surrender to horrible conviction of the Holy Spirit.

Here is an excerpt of the effects of revival and sin:
The revivalists of the early 19th Century, men such as Presbyterian Charles Finney, used the "mourner's bench" or "anxious seat" to encourage members of the audience to truly repent. Finney wrote,
When sinners and backsliders are really convicted by the Holy Ghost, they are greatly ashamed of themselves. Until they manifest deep shame, it should be known that the probe is not used sufficiently, and they do not see themselves as they ought. When I go into a meeting of inquiry and look over the multitudes,

if I see them with heads up, looking at me and at each other, I have learned to understand what work I have to do. Instead of pressing them immediately to come to Christ, I must go to work to convict them of sin. Generally, by looking over the room, a minister can easily tell, not only who are convicted and who are not, but who are so deeply convicted as to be prepared to receive Christ. Some are looking around and manifest no shame at all; others cannot look you in the face and yet can hold up their heads; others still cannot hold up their heads and yet are silent; others by their sobbing, and breathing, and agonizing, reveal at once the fact that the sword of the Spirit has wounded them to their very heart. . . . [There must be] that kind of genuine and deep conviction which breaks the sinner and the backslider right down and makes him unutterably ashamed and confounded before the Lord, until he is not only stripped of every excuse, but driven to go all lengths in justifying God and condemning himself.

Charles G. Finney, Reflections on Revival, ed. Donald W. Dayton. (Minneapolis, MN: Bethany House Publishers, 1979), 16-17, quoted here.

Ephesians 5:1-16
1 Be ye therefore followers of God, as dear children.
2 And walk-in love, as Christ also hath loved us, and hath given himself for us an offering and a sacrifice to God for a sweet-smelling savour.

3 But fornication, and all uncleanness, or covetousness, let it not be once named among you, as becometh saints;

4 Neither filthiness, nor foolish talking, nor jesting, which are not convenient: but rather giving of thanks.

5 For this ye know, that no whoremonger, nor unclean person, nor covetous man, who is an idolater, hath any inheritance in the kingdom of Christ and of God.

6 Let no man deceive you with vain words: for because of these things cometh the wrath of God upon the children of disobedience.

7 Be not ye therefore partakers with them.

8 For ye were sometimes darkness, but now are ye light in the Lord: walk as children of light:

9 (For the fruit of the Spirit is in all goodness and righteousness and truth;)

10 Proving what is acceptable unto the Lord.

11 And have no fellowship with the unfruitful works of darkness, but rather reprove them.

12 For it is a shame even to speak of those things which are done of them in secret.

13 But all things that are reproved are made manifest by the light: for whatsoever doth make manifest is light.

14 Wherefore he saith, Awake thou that sleepest, and arise from the dead, and Christ shall give thee light.

15 See then that ye walk circumspectly, not as fools, but as wise,

16 Redeeming the time, because the days are evil.

Perilous Times: Idolatry of Self

Perhaps you are wanting to know what the future holds as 2020 was a difficult year we all want just to go away. However, 2020 revealed some deep level issues which simply will not go away with the turning of the calendar. Some of the more revealing moments were when human nature was brought to the forefront for all to see. The level of corruption and lies runs deeper than what others want to admit and just correct itself. So, what is really unfolding as we go into a new year? The Bible teaches a moral decline in the last days, along with an increase in lawlessness. Ironically in the last days as mankind advances in knowledge and technology the nature of corruption is brought out into fullness. We are entering into times which the Bible describes as perilous times.

What is the main problem? Men are lovers of themselves. Who would have thought that self-love would be the peril of the last days? It actually makes sense though, in the Scriptures mankind's temptation is to be his own god. As the Second Coming of the Lord approaches, we see the age of man arising, we want a man to save the world. Of course, the only man capable of saving the world is being despised and rejected, as fallen man refuse Salvation in Jesus Christ alone. As the result we see the powerful influences which drives men to self-absorption, and the world of self-love. Man creates an image of himself which is an idol based upon the world's values. The peril of the last days is man has become an idol unto himself, man can save the world without the help of God. The more the idolatry of man is celebrated the more the corrupt nature of man comes to the forefront. Man is now in the deep corruption of worshiping the image of man.

What will be the outcome of man worshiping his own image? The most perilous outcome is a departure from worshipping and loving God. All which idolatry of man becomes is self-worship. Even now you can see these very tendencies in the organized Church. The peril among Christians is to hold to a form of Godliness without the character of Jesus Christ. The Church of man has arisen, and it is all about you, and what makes you happy. The Golden Calf of manmade worship the idol of self has moved the Church from Christ centrality to where it is all about me, my wants, and my feelings, and my desires. The Church has fallen to singing about themselves and calling it worship. The Church has fallen to a false Gospel which promises the world and speaks nothing of the Cross.

Where are we going? The image of the beautified man is being put on display. Idolatry is being played out in the sexual arena. Homosexuality, adultery, fornication, and all manner of sexual imagery has captured the Imagination of the world. The floodgate has been opened to the idolatry of sex, and you can see it's progression from the 1940's to the outright celebration of sexual immorality of today. Today's image of a modern women is almost naked with nothing left to the imagination as the female body is celebrated in its sexuality. The outward appearances of moral chastity and purity have nothing to do with modern culture. A man is not celebrated for purity of heart or moral character, instead what idolized image one can create through sexual exploitation and physical enhancement are what culture idolizes. Soon all sexual restraints will have fallen to the ground and all of culture will have adopted sexual perversion as the normal course of life. Sex will demonstrate how much a man idolizes and loves himself and care little or nothing for the love of God. The peril of the days we live in, are as in the Days of Lot in Sodom just before fire and brimstone rained down from heaven. Man is certainly in love with his naked body and no longer has any remorse or shame for his lust for sexual perversion.

The more man idolizes Himself, the more we see deep level corruption. As deep darkness advances upon the earth the opposite of Gods moral character and truth will be celebrated. Lies will become the truth, light will be called darkness, and darkness the light. Good will be called evil, and evil will be called good. On the outside man will appear to himself as wise and beautiful, on the inside all manner of wickedness and corruption. How can we escape for because of these things the wrath of God is coming upon the world? Will men admit the idolatry of self has drawn the wrath of God? Ironically, these days are also like the days of Noah right before the great deluge of waters. Men will be so wise in their own eyes they will have discarded the fear of the Lord as fairy tales. What brings the final judgments of God, the denial of God and the worship of man's own image. The colossal man, the golden image is being put on display. All over the world men are being commanded to bow down to the golden image of man. At the sound of music man must now down and worship man. As a trap upon the whole world has come the temptation for a man to be his own God. Will man then return to the Garden of Eden once again and make for a utopian world? Many in the Church are proclaiming a worldwide Church takeover. These men are lovers of themselves and not lovers of the truth. Wicked men and imposters are waxing word and worse in the Church.

How do we escape the great snare which has come upon the whole world? We refuse to bow down and are willing to be cast into the fiery furnace. As we bow our not or knees to any image of man no matter how many people who call themselves Christian have loved their golden image of self.

2 Timothy 3:1-10
1 This know also, that in the
last days perilous times shall come.
2 For men shall be lovers of their own
selves, covetous, boasters, proud, blasphemers, disobed
ient to parents, unthankful, unholy,

3 Without natural affection, trucebreakers, false
accusers, incontinent, fierce, despisers of those that are
good,
4 Traitors, heady, high minded, lovers of
pleasures more than lovers of God;
5 Having a form of godliness, but denying the
power thereof: from such turn away.
6 For of this sort are they which
creep into houses, and lead captive silly
women laden with sins, led away with divers lusts,
7 Ever learning, and never able to come to the
knowledge of the truth.
8 Now as Jannes and Jambres withstood Moses, so do t
hese also resist the truth: men of corrupt
minds, reprobate concerning the faith.
9 But they shall proceed no further: for their folly shall
be manifest unto all men, as theirs also was.
10 But thou hast fully known my doctrine, manner of
life, purpose, faith, longsuffering, charity, patience,

Chapter Five
Practical Acts

Giving No Oath

Matthew 5:33-37
33 Again, ye have heard that it hath been said by them
of old time, Thou shalt not forswear thyself, but shalt
perform unto the Lord thine oaths:
34 But I say unto you, Swear not at
all; neither by heaven; for it is God's throne:

35 Nor by the earth; for it
is his footstool: neither by Jerusalem; for it is the city of
the great King.
36 Neither shalt thou swear by thy head, because thou
canst not make one hair white or black.
37 But let your communication be, Yea, yea; Nay, nay: f
or whatsoever is more than these cometh of evil.

Excerpt From Robert Govett

In these words, our Lord seems to have in His eye the
third and the ninth commandments.

He is forbidding Oaths. What is an oath ?

1 . It is often said, that ' calling God to witness ' is an
oath. This is part of an oath : but, taken by itself it is not
so.

2. It is rightly defined by Barnes thus : " An oath is a
solemn affirmation or declaration made with an appeal
to God for the truth of what is affirmed, and
imprecating His vengeance and renouncing His favor , if
what is affirmed is false" Or as another has described it
more briefly, it is — (1) self-binding, (2) under self-
imprecation.

The oath in English courts of justice is as follows : " The
evidence you shall give to the court and jury sworn,
between our Sovereign Lady the Queen and the
prisoner at the bar, shall be the truth, the whole truth,

and nothing but the truth ; so, help you God ! " Where-
upon the New Testament is kissed, as a sign that the
oath is taken. That word, — ' So help you God,' contains
the imprecation. It is as if you said, — ' If I speak
anything but the truth, may God at the day of judgment
give me no help to escape His wroth ! * That is, — 'May
I be damned ! *"

The Sermon On the Mount Expounded; pages 91 and
92: Robert Govett.

The basic issue of giving an oath is to put yourself under
a judgment which would exclude you from God's grace,
or not in Gods will. Why would a disciple of Jesus Christ
put himself under a position where he cannot perform
the will of God for their lives? Instead of compromising
with God by giving a pledge or oath, Christ warns His
disciples not to make the oath in the first place.

Christ instructed His disciples not to swear at all, even if
were in the name of God or by heaven and Gods
Throne. Even if we were to swear by things on earth or
pledge our head if we failed to keep our oath. The Lord
stresses a person cannot even make one hair black or
white, so our confidence should only be in God, and not
our abilities. Our speech and conduct should
demonstrate our complete relance, and dependence on
God alone. If we go beyond in our communication were
shall surely fall into what is evil. Let your
communication be yes or no for those very reasons.

Love Your Enemies

Jesus Christ contrasts the Old Testament law, with the commands of Christ required for His disciples. In the Old Testament the law required retribution for justice. An eye for an eye, a tooth for a tooth. Equal justice for all who would break Old Testament laws.

Matthew 5:38-48

38 Ye have heard that it hath been said, An eye for an eye, and a tooth for a tooth:
39 But I say unto you, That ye
resist not evil: but whosoever shall
smite thee on thy right cheek, turn to the other also.

However, the Sermon On the Mount requires of His disciples a deeper Christ like suffering from injustices. Those who serve the Lord must understand unjust suffering will come, but our response to those injustices is vitally important. The Lord requires the disciples not to retaliate against evil; "But I say unto you, That you resist not evil." Without the indwelling Holy Spirit our natural response is self-defense. "But whosoever smite you on your right cheek, turn to the other also." Those who do not resist evil must be fully submitted to the Lord, trusting Gods ultimate judgment with Him.

Matthew 5:20-41

40 And if any man will sue thee at the law, and take
away thy coat, let him have thy cloke also.
41 And whosoever shall compel thee to
go a mile, go with him twain.

The unjust suffering of the saints also includes the loss
of one's personal goods, and possessions. The world will
make laws against the Lord and His disciples and bring
them before their courts and magistrates. As justice in
man's court of law often violates Gods laws, the
Disciples of Jesus Christ must be willing to suffer unjust
loss by man's court of law. Being wrongly sued, the loss
of personal goods and security. If they take your coat,
let them have your cloak too. Whoever goes to a great
length to destroy your life because of your testimony of
the Lord, be willing to go twice the distance in standing
with the Lord entrusting your justice into His hands.

Matthew 5:42
42 Give to him that asketh thee, and from him that
would borrow of thee turn not thou away.

When anyone has a real need, and you have the
provision the Lord requires His disciples to give to that
need. The Lord expects His disciples to go out of the
normal way in giving to the needs of others.

Matthew 5:43-44
43 Ye have heard that it hath been said, Thou shalt

love thy neighbour, and hate thine enemy.
44 But I say unto you, Love your enemies, bless them
that curse you, do good to them that
hate you, and pray for them which despitefully
use you, and persecute you;

Now comes some of the most difficult commands of the
whole Sermon On the Mount. It requires great resolve
for Christ's disciples to surrender their wills to the will of
God. God says in Old Testament law you shall love your
neighbor and hate your enemy. Now the Lord lays down
His commands of love, so contrary to the rest of the
world. But I say unto you (Disciples) love your enemies.
How can any man without God's grace be able to love
his enemy? Bless them which curse you, do good to
them which hate you. Only God can fulfill these
commands in your life. In no way can a natural man
have these desires in himself. These deep love
commands require a deep surrender to Jesus Christ.

Matthew 5:35
45 That ye may be the children of your Father which
is in heaven: for he maketh his sun to rise on the
evil and on the good, and sendeth rain on the
just and on the unjust.

The fulfillment of these commands demonstrate the
Disciples of Christ are children born from above, and
God is their Father. As God in His benevolence causes
his sun to rise on the evil and the good. God supplies his

goodness even to those who are wicked and unjust. Even the wicked are supplied with the sun and rain to feed themselves.

The love commands reveal future rewards for all who are willing to obey them and suffer loss in this age.

Matthew 5:46
46 For if ye love them which
love you, what reward have ye? do not even the
publicans the same?

What reward with God do you have if you only love those who love you?

There is no reward in you love only those who will love you back. Instead, you are to love your enemies, which no common man will naturally do. In this way the Disciples of Christ demonstrate a nature which shines before men and brings glory to God our Father.

47 And if ye
salute your brethren only, what do ye more than others? do not even the publicans so?

Finally, God requires us to surrender to His will in obedience to His love commands. No man can be perfect without sin like Jesus Christ. However, according to Gods will, perfect love can be perfected in the disciples of Christ. We can love according to the commands of Christ. In this way Gods perfect love can be matured and perfected by the saints of God.

Matthew 5:48
48 Be ye therefore perfect, even as your Father which is in heaven is perfect.

The Greek word here translated "perfect" is "teleios is not perfect as without fault. Instead, the word perfect in these passages could be translated mature, or of full age. A disciple of Christ who has followed these love commands has grown and matured in love. Any man who is willing to put the love commands of Christ will grow up in Christ likeness. As the Book of Ephesians demonstrates God is wanting to raise mature sons who are growing into to the stature of the fullness which belongs to Christ.

Ephesians 4:13-16
13 Till we all come in the unity of the faith, and of the knowledge of the Son of God, unto perfect man, unto the measure of the stature of the fulness of Christ:
14 That we henceforth be no more children, tossed to and fro, and carried about with every wind of doctrine, by the sleight of men, and cunning craftiness, whereby they lie in wait to deceive;
15 But speaking the truth in love, may grow up into him in all things, which is the head, even Christ:
16 From whom the whole body fitly joined

together and compacted by that
which every joint supplieth, according to the effectual
working in the measure of
every part, maketh increase of the body unto the
edifying of itself in love.

Chapter Six
Giving To God and Heavenly Treasure

One of the most important aspects of Christs teachings
His disciples in the Sermon On the Mount has to do with
giving and laying up your treasures in heaven. In order
to receive Kingdom age entrance and rewards disciples
of Christ must be willing to give to God in secret. Jesus
Christ warns for His disciples not to give alms, deeds of
benevolence, to be seen before men. In giving to
receive glory and praise from men your motives for
giving have been corrupted. When you give to be seen
of men, you have forfeited your right of rewards which
come from God the Father alone.

Once again, the issue of hypocrisy is addressed, when
religious leaders in the days of Jesus Christs earthly
ministry would make sure in the synagogues, they
sounded a trumpet to bring notice to themselves when
doing alms. Even in the modern organized Church many
ministries want to draw disciples unto themselves, so as
to benefit when men are glorying in "how much they
serve and give to God." In reality they want to be seen
of men to receive their praise and have corrupted

motives in their giving. Jesus Christ warns His disciples of this hypocrisy, warning these hypocrites have received their reward from men, but will have none from God.

Jesus Christ then instructs His disciples on how to give alms in secret so other men do not know what you are doing. "When you give alms let not your left hand know what your right hand does." The disciple in Christ must serve the Lord often in hidden ways out of the view of men, not seen by men or praised for your goodness. When alms are done in secret God the Father sees, and His disciple is trust for future rewards from God, and not coming from men. Your compromise with God in hypocrisy will cause disqualification for Kingdom age rewards at the Judgment Seat of Christ.

Matthew 6:1-4
1 Take heed that ye do not your alms before men, to be seen of them: otherwise ye have no reward
of your Father which is in heaven.
2 Therefore when thou doest thine alms, do not sound a trumpet before thee, as the hypocrites do in the synagogues and in the streets, that they may have glory of men. Verily I say unto you, They have their reward.
3 But when thou doest alms, let not thy left hand know what thy right hand doeth:
4 That thine alms may

be in secret: and thy Father which
seeth in secret himself shall reward thee openly.

Prayer In Secret

The hidden life of devotion is highly emphasized by
Jesus Christ in the Sermon On the Mount. In the
previous passages Christ taught His disciples to give in
secret out of sight from the praise of men. Giving to
receive the praise and advantage of men, demonstrates
corrupted motives and hypocrisy. Now the same
standards are applied to a secret prayer life. Hypocrites
in the days of Jesus Christ liked to use prayer in public to
be seen of men as spiritual and exalted in their eyes.
Prayer from Christs disciples must not be motivated by
the need to be praised by man. A true life of devotion
has deeply embedded into the disciple's life a hidden
life of prayer. Out of the view of men is the authentic
prayer life of a man devoted to Jesus Christ. When a
man prays in secret, behind closed doors heaven hears
and rewards. Prayer life has great value in service to the
Lord and carries great rewards not only in this present
evil age, but rewards given by Christ for the coming
Kingdom of heaven age. A man who prays in secret will
be rewarded openly before men by the Lord.

Once again Jesus Christ warns of hypocritical motives
even in prayer. Praying to be seen has corrupted
motives, the need to receive praise of men. How the
true saint of God hides himself in the prayer closet,

away from the busy noise of religion. Prayer in secret moves heaven and gives the servant of the Lord place with God. A prayer in secret is one whom God will hear, and this man will move heaven by his passion to bring glory to God in prayer. "But when you pray enter into your closet, and shut your door, pray to the Father which is in secret, and the Father which sees in secret shall reward you openly."

The effectual fervent prayer of a righteous man avails much with God. For when you pray do not use scripted prayer in vain repetitions, for this is the practice of the religions who know not God. For those who do not know God think they will be heard for their multitude of words. These are not prayers of faith, instead are coming from unbelief and self-will. God does not lead His disciples to pray after this manner. For God, our Father knows what we need even before we ask in prayer. Our confidence is in our Lord God alone, and prayer in secret is a demonstration of our faith and reliance in Him.

Matthew 6:5-8
5 And when thou prayest, thou shalt not be as the hypocrites are: for they love to pray standing in the synagogues and in the corners of the
streets, that they may be seen of men. Verily I say unto you, They have their reward.
6 But thou, when thou

prayest, enter into thy closet, and when thou hast
shut thy door, pray to thy Father which
is in secret; and thy Father which seeth in secret shall
reward thee openly.
7 But when ye pray, use not vain repetitions, as the
heathen do: for they think that they shall be heard
for their much speaking.
8 **Be** not ye therefore like unto
them: for your Father knoweth what things ye
have need of, before ye ask him.

The Lord's Prayer
9 After this manner therefore pray ye: Our Father which
art in heaven, Hallowed be thy name.
10 Thy kingdom come. Thy will be done in earth, as it
is in heaven.
11 Give us this day our daily bread.
12 And forgive us our debts, as we forgive our debtors.
13 And lead us not into temptation, but deliver us from
evil: For thine is the kingdom, and the power, and the
glory, forever. Amen.

In no way is the Lord's Prayer about the Church bringing
the Kingdom of Heaven to earth before the Second
Coming of Jesus Christ. Instead fitting with the themes
of the Sermon On the Mount, the Lord's Prayer is all
about seeking and depending on God in this present evil
age. As the Lord has instructed the saints to put the
Lord first in their lives, and Christ would add those

things which are necessary for life. So, in the Lord's Prayer we see requests which fit the facts of Christians completely depending on God to meet their needs. In contrast to the Gentiles seeking for these things which keeps them in bondage to the world system. Putting Christ first in your life frees you from fear to live after the love commands of the Sermon On the Mount.

The Lord instructed His disciples after this manner pray:

1) Our Father Which art in heaven.
   Prayer is to God the Father who rules from the heaven of heavens. The saints who are born of the Spirit are to pray to God as their Father. Which by spiritual birth makes them children of God. Making God responsible to Father His sons would by His nature make provision for all their needs.
2) Hallowed Be Your name

Part of prayer is also praise and worship. God holds the highest position of glory far above all His creation. When the Scriptures reveal the heavenly scene all of God's creatures, the heavenly host cry out in adoration and praise. The same goes for God's children who worship God in Spirit and truth. God is seeking worshipers who give Him all the glory. Also demonstrate their love for Him by keeping His commandments.

3) Your Kingdom Come

Much has to be said of the coming Kingdom of Heaven on earth. The Kingdom of Heaven is future at the Second Coming of Jesus Christ. The commands of the Lord make the saints to seek first the Kingdom of Heaven making their life a pilgrimage in this present evil age. The saint's home is future, as they look for Gods will to be done on earth as it is in heaven.

4) Your Will be done on earth as it is in heaven. Simply put, this age is in rebellion to God. A fallen age, under the curse of sin and death. Praying for the will of God requires perseverance now, and faith for the fulfillment of Gods promises many which will not be fully answered in this age. God will answer many prayers of the saints now, however complete redemption will require the next age also.

5) Give us our daily bread.
   Prayer also requires dependence on God to meet our basic needs. When you seek first the Kingdom, God will add all these things unto you. Food, clothing, housing, God has promised to provide when you have put Him first in your life. Your surrender to God often times will put you in position where you are in need. Trusting God

means you continue to serve the Lord and pray to God to meet your needs. Even when it looks like the circumstances are contrary and could not happen without God's intervention. Prayer, then is the recognition of your needs before God. Who is your source and supply as you continue to trust His will for your life?

6) And forgive our debts, as we forgive our debtors. How important is forgives to the disciples of Jesus Christ. Holding onto another's debut or offense puts us at odds with the Lord. Here is another set of Scriptures which supports the necessity for forgiving other debts, even as the Lord has forgiven ours.

Matthew 18:21-35
21 Then came Peter to him, and said, Lord, how oft shall my brother sin against me, and I forgive him? till seven times?
22 Jesus saith unto him, I say not unto thee, Until seven times: but, Until seventy times seven.
23 Therefore is the kingdom of heaven likened unto a certain king, which would take account of his servants.
24 And when he had begun to reckon, one was brought unto him, which owed him ten thousand talents.

25 But forasmuch as he had not to
pay, his lord commanded him to be
sold, and his wife, and children, and all that he
had, and payment to be made.
26 The servant therefore fell down, and
worshipped him, saying, Lord, have
patience with me, and I will pay thee all.
27 Then the lord of that servant was moved with
compassion, and loosed him, and forgave him the debt.
28 But the same servant went out, and
found one of his fellow servants, which owed him an
hundred pence: and he laid hands on him, and
took him by the throat, saying, Pay me that thou owest.
29 And his fellow servant fell down at his feet, and
besought him, saying, Have patience with me, and I will
pay thee all.
30 And he would not: but went
and cast him into prison, till he should pay the debt.
31 So when his fellow servants saw what was done, they
were very sorry, and came and told unto
their lord all that was done.
32 Then his lord, after that he had called him, said unto
him, O thou wicked servant, I forgave thee all
that debt, because thou desiredst me:
33 Shouldest not thou also have had
compassion on thy fellow servant, even as I had pity on
thee?
34 And his lord was worth, and delivered him to the
tormentors, till he should pay all that was due unto him.
35 So likewise shall my heavenly Father do also unto

you, if ye from your hearts forgive not everyone
his brother their trespasses.

7) And lead us not in temptation but deliver us
   from evil.

The saints born of the Spirit must be led of the Spirit.
Even though they have been given forgiveness of sins,
and a new nature many trials will be set their walk of
faith. As the world system is set against the saints , all
who follow the Lord must pick up the Cross in self-
denial and fellowship in the sufferings of Christ. For all
disciples of the Lord who would follow after
righteousness will suffer persecution for their faith. As
the Kingdoms of this present evil age are yet under the
bondage to the Prince of the Power of the Air. In
response the saints must resist the devil and draw near
to God. As the result of Satanic trials and temptations
prayer for deliverance from evil will be a very necessary
part of walking through the fire and through the flood.

8) For yours is the Kingdom, and the power, and
   the glory.

Prayer is also affirmation of things not seen. As the
whole world lies in the power of the evil one
deliverance from Satan is still future. Even though the
Cross and Resurrection of Jesus Christ has already paid
the price of redemption, the Day of Redemption our full
deliverance is still future. The saints must walk with

faith and patience to inherit the promises of God. Keeping your heart right before the Lord by prayer and supplication acknowledging Christs Kingdom, power, and glory are promised in fulness in the future. Though it tarries the promise is sure as God cannot lie and cannot fail.

9) Forever, Amen.

The Kingdom, power and glory are the Lords and will never pass away. So be it. Prayer stands in the triumph of Christ. Praying back to God what He has promised by His word and will.

Making Jesus Christ First In Your Life

Modern Christianity is challenged with making Jesus Christ the Lord. So many Christians are struggling to make Jesus Christ first in their lives. When Christians are not living for the Lord, the Bible has very little relevance for their lives. Let us face it, the study of the Scriptures is not a priority in the lives of modern Christians. Without the Bible as the word of final authority, Christians are struggling with their flesh, not walking in victory over sin, and living for the things of the world. Modern Christianity, is all about feeling good, feeling sympathetic with God's love, but lacks real substance when having to walk in obedience, a real surrendered life to Christ. It is like if you are saved, you once had zeal for the Lord, you would pray, study the Bible with a hunger to learn more about God, and you wanted to be with other Christians. However, now days your love has grown cold, you do not seek the Lord anymore, and you are cut off from real relationships with other Christians. I trust the condition speaks of a Church in a major decline, moving away from the authentic faith into a counterfeit Christianity.

How would Christians get back to putting Jesus Christ first in their lives? First you must make a major decision to walk with Jesus Christ as the Lord of life. His will has first place, you must deny yourself and seek God's will for your life. What does this mean? Seeking first the Kingdom of God, putting your life, your needs, what you are living for into the hands of God. Your time is important to God, you must redeem your time for the days are evil. Realize you are in a spiritual battle with evil. With the Kingdom of Darkness evil malevolent spirits who resists your walk in the Lord. Notice the moment you make a quality decision to live for the Lord temptation and resistance will come. If you truly live for Jesus Christ in this present evil age, expect a spiritual battle over your life, trials, tests, and temptations will come your way. The battle is not with flesh and blood instead evil spirits in the kingdom of darkness want to war against your life in Christ. You must make Jesus Christ your refuge and being willing to suffer for the faith.

A genuine prayer life will be required in order to overcome the evil day. Seeking the Lord on a daily basis in prayer as a real refuge, being strengthen by the Lord to face very real battles. Coming to know the Lord by a real working of the Cross in your life. Just like when you saw the value of the Cross the first time. The Cross does not lose any efficacy now that many years have passed, the Cross has just as much value throughout all eternity. You must confess your sins before God, get your heart right seeking the Lord knowing your life is crucified with Christ. The Blood of Jesus Christ has great significance in spiritual battles with sin, the flesh, and evil spirits. The Blood answers the accusations of conscience, and the accuser of the brethren when you are living in sin, and not living right with God. The blood of Jesus Christ is God's answer for our sin, for without the shedding of blood there is no remission of sins. To get back in real fellowship with the Lord, all sin, all things which accuse us before the Lord must be put into the Cross. Forgiveness must come from the blood, real confession before the Lord until you are cleansed from all unrighteousness.

Modern Christianity knows little of the Cross, speaks and teaches little of the Blood of Christ. So much is fantasy Christianity make believe spiritual warfare, and pretend conquest and victory. Young Christians are feed a diet of spiritual highs, learning to "feel God," but do not know the Cross or the Blood. What happens when all the "good feelings, or God feelings stop?" You must live by faith trusting the Cross, the power of the Blood, even when circumstance our feelings tell you God is nowhere in sight. It is time Christians get back to Jesus Christ seeking the Lord daily and applying the Blood of the Cross in real cleansing and forgiveness. When the conscience is free from accusations, you are resting in the power of the Blood Sacrifice and have entered into real communion with the Lord. If we say we have no sin, we walk in darkness and the darkness has blinded our eyes. So many Christians are self-deceived living in sin, and still saying they have fellowship with God.

Time to get right. Confess your sins and seek God until the Blood of Christ cleanses you from all unrighteousness. You cannot hold onto your life of sin, and still walk with the Lord. Time to put Jesus Christ first in your life and put the Cross back into your walk of faith.

1 John 1
1 That which was from the beginning, which we have heard, which we have seen with our eyes, which we have looked upon, and our hands have handled, of the Word of life.
2 (For the life was manifested, and we have seen it, and bear witness, and shew unto you that eternal life, which was with the Father, and was manifested unto us;)
3 That which we have seen and heard declare we unto you, that ye also may have fellowship with us: and truly our fellowship is with the Father, and with his Son Jesus Christ.

4 And these things write we unto you, that your joy may be full.

5 This then is the message which we have heard of him, and declare unto you, that God is light, and in him is no darkness at all.

6 If we say that we have fellowship with him, and walk-in darkness, we lie, and do not the truth:

7 But if we walk in the light, as he is in the light, we have fellowship one with another, and the blood of Jesus Christ his Son cleanseth us from all sin.

8 If we say that we have no sin, we deceive ourselves, and the truth is not in us.

9 If we confess our sins, he is faithful and just to forgive us our sins, and to cleanse us from all unrighteousness.

10 If we say that we have not sinned, we make him a liar, and his word is not in us.

Chapter Seven
Seeking First the Kingdom of Heaven

Matthew 6:33

33 But seek ye first the kingdom of God, and his righteousness; and all these things added unto.

34 Take therefore no thought for the morrow: for the morrow shall take thought for the things of itself. Sufficient unto the day is the evil thereof

What does it mean for Disciples of Jesus Christ to seek first the Kingdom of God, and His righteousness? What Are You Seeking?

The Sermon On the Mount is a major overview of the Christian life. One of the great emphasis in the Sermon On the Mount is in seeking. Which means a looking forward, Jesus Christ commanded the Church not to seek first food, clothing, and housing. Unbelievers want to seek out those things and build their lives around them. The emphasis seems to be on seeking the things of the Lord which are contrary to this present age. The disciples of Christ are on a pilgrimage towards a coming age which has the rule of Christ. The next age is called the Kingdom of Heaven, and the disciples of Christ are commanded to seek first the coming Kingdom of Heaven putting the things of the world in the trust of the Lord. For when you seek first the Lordship of Jesus Christ, then the Lord directs your profession, the place you live, and the things which are necessary for your service to Him.

The path of the righteous is extremely narrow and very restrictive. The Sermon On the Mount described the path towards the Kingdom as a straight gate and a narrow way. When you follow the Lord, you are on the straight and narrow way with many of the world's seductions tempting you to follow the Broadway unto destruction. You must ask yourself what are you seeking? For what do you give your time, talents, and pursuit? As you cannot just do your own life, and then expect to be rewarded with the Lord's blessing. The danger to the disciples of Christ is not to continue in the straight and narrow way towards the coming Kingdom age. The disciple's life is one of pilgrimage towards the Second Coming of Jesus Christ, and the Kingdom of Heaven on earth. The cost of following the Lord is to pick up the Cross in self-denial and live for the Lord, and not the things of the world.

Staying on the narrow way, the path the Lord has set before us is extremely difficult. Keeping Christ first in your life will require the sacrifice of your will and desires. The Lord teaches in the Sermon On the Mount you cannot serve two masters for you will love the one and hate the other, you will hold to the one and despise the other. The problem being when disciples begin to build their own kingdoms laying up treasures here on earth which have temporal rewards. Sadly, a false Gospel has invaded the Church which makes the worlds treasures the blessing of the Lord. Christians has grown cold and compromised under the false Gospel of Kingdom building. As it leads the saints away from the straight and narrow way.

In order to stay in the narrow way Jesus Christ teaches in the Sermon On the Mount how to pray in secret, and not to be seen of men. How to fast from food in order to seek the Lord, and not too fast to be seen of men. So much of what goes on in the name of the Lord is the pursuit of seeking glory from men. One of the great hindrances, the great temptations with the Lords disciples is to see glory which comes from men, and not the glory which comes from the Lord. So much of what is called the glory of the Lord, is nothing more than man made glorification. The cheap tinsel of sensuous manifestations are being celebrated by men seeking glory for their own ministries. How cheap is the way of men that sell the Church out for cheap manifestations, and declare it to be God's glory? The real gold is found in picking up the Cross and keeping in the true seeking of Kingdom glory. The prize of the high calling rewarded with the glory found in Christ will not be found in this age. For those who have sold out with man's glorification have their cheap imitation and reward now.

Here is the warning for those disciples who have sold out to the fame and glory of the world. Only those who seek first the Kingdom are qualified to enter the Kingdom of Heaven at the end of this age. The Sermon On the Mount warns of Kingdom forfeiture, being disinherited by not measuring up to the Lords demands in the Sermon. Jesus Christ warned not everyone who says to Me Lord Lord shall enter the Kingdom of Heaven. Two big mistakes are made by modern beliefs in this passage. First not to believe the passage is a warning to born again Christians. Second to make the loss of the Kingdom to mean these disciples were never saved in the first place. Instead of what Jesus Christ warned of throughout the whole of the Sermon On the Mount. You shall not inherit means; you cannot enter the Kingdom age because you sold out your birth right for the temporary pleasures of sin and the world. The Broadway of destruction is the path of the masses and it will lead you to seek the things of the world. The straight and narrow way which few find will lead you to the Kingdom age rewards and glory.

Kingdom Increase Or Decrease

"Of the increase of His government and peace there shall be no end..." It has become popular within the Charismatic political camp to teach an ever-increasing government. Those of the apostolic/prophetic persuasion follow the philosophical belief the knowledge of the Glory of the Lord is being spread as the Kingdom of Heaven all over the world by the Church. So popular has become this philosophy, new terminology has developed around it called the 7 Mountain Mandate. The basic belief is by marketplace apostles and prophets of the Charismatic Church will cleanse the 7 pillars of culture, thereby Christianizing the nations before Jesus Christ can return. The belief is an ever-increasing apostolic government which will fill the whole earth. In this doctrine there is no place for a weak and defeated Church. Names like Joel's Army speak of an end time super Church and worldwide take over.

However, is this the record of Scriptures? An ever-increasing Glorious Church able to spread the Kingdom of heaven, the Government of God all over the earth before the Second Coming? This might be surprising to many Charismatic's who have been taught the "Kingdom of heaven to earth" philosophy, but the Scriptures do not support an end time Church worldwide take over. At best, the Church will experience a "complete mixture" of righteousness and corruption. The Parable of the Wheat and Tares proves they grow side by side in this age until the Second Coming of Jesus Christ. In fact, the prediction of a "transformed culture" by cleansing the 7 pillars is "nowhere to be found in Scriptures." It is a dream made up by human philosophy, a looking for a Christian Utopia on earth before the Second Coming of Jesus Christ. Sadly, other religions which are not based in the Christian faith also are looking for the same thing, as well as many worldly philosophies. Now here is a warning from Jesus Christ about the end of the age and world peace: (1 Thessalonians 5:1-3)

"But of the times and the seasons, brethren, ye have no need that I write unto you. For yourselves know perfectly that the day of the Lord so cometh as a thief in the night.

For when they shall say, Peace and safety; then sudden destruction cometh upon them, as travail upon a woman with child; and they shall not escape."

Did you get that? About the time the world has believed it has achieved worldwide peace comes the time of the "Tribulation." A time in which Jesus Christ describes as the "greatest trial" the world will ever see or know. (Matthew 24:21-22)
"For then shall be great tribulation, such as was not since the beginning of the world to this time, no, nor ever shall be. And except those days should be shortened, there should no flesh be saved: but for the elect's sake those days shall be shortened."

Why would the signs and wonders Charismatic Movement reject the counsel of Scriptures and teach the false doctrine of an end time Super Church? Why would the Charismatic Movement teach that end time super apostles will restore proper Church government and Christianize the world before Jesus Christ can return. Clearly, the world's worst trial did not happen in 33 AD, (Cross) or 70 AD the destruction of the Temple by General Titus of Rome. Neither has the Church in 2000 years of Church history made the government of the Church transform even one city, or nation into the "government of God on earth." There has been no increase of removal of evil, or the dethronement of Satan as years of Charismatic doctrine teach.

Let us look at simple Scriptures which warn of an end time decline in the Church. The exact opposite message from Scriptures from what is being preached by the apostolic Movement today. Just a small sampling of straight forward warnings of an end time Church decline.

Also notice the Scriptures warn of the spread of the Antichrist government all over the world before Jesus Christ returns. Not a worldwide take over by the Church, in fact just the opposite.

1) An Increase in false doctrines and teachers inside the Church. Doctrines which come from the influences of evil spirits, called philosophies in Scripture.

1 Timothy 4:1
1 Now the Spirit speaketh expressly, that in the latter times some shall depart from the faith, giving heed to seducing spirits, and doctrines of devils.

2 Timothy 4:3-4
3 For the time will come when they will not endure sound doctrine; but after their own lusts shall they heap to themselves teachers, having itching ears.
4 And they shall turn away their ears from the truth and shall be turned unto fables.

2) Wicked Leaders Inside the Church

2 Timothy 3:13

13 But evil men and seducers shall wax worse and worse, deceiving, and being deceived.

3) Perilous Times

2 Timothy 3:1-8

1 This know also, that in the last days perilous times shall come.

2 For men shall be lovers of their own selves, covetous, boasters, proud, blasphemers, disobedient to parents, unthankful, unholy,

3 Without natural affection, trucebreakers, false accusers, incontinent, fierce, despisers of those that are good,

4 Traitors, heady, high minded, lovers of pleasures more than lovers of God.

5 Having a form of godliness but denying the power thereof: from such turn away.

6 For of this sort are they which creep into houses, and lead captive silly women laden with sins, led away with divers' lusts,

7 Ever learning, and never able to come to the knowledge of the truth.

8 Now as Jannes and Jambres withstood Moses, so do these also resist the truth: men of corrupt minds, reprobate concerning the faith.

4) A Great Apostasy From the Faith

2 Thessalonians 2:1-5

1 Now we beseech you, brethren, by the coming of our Lord Jesus Christ, and by our gathering together unto him,

2 That ye be not soon shaken in mind, or be troubled, neither by spirit, nor by word, nor by letter as from us, as that the day of Christ is at hand.

3 Let no man deceive you by any means: for that day shall not come, except there comes a falling away first, and that man of sin be revealed, the son of perdition.

4 Who opposeth and exalteth himself above all that is called God, or that is worshipped; so that he as God sitteth in the temple of God, shewing himself that he is God.

5 Remember ye not, that, when I was yet with you, I told you these things?

    5)   A Decline In Morality, Not Purification of Culture Luke 17:26-32

26 And as it was in the days of Noe, so shall it be also in the days of the Son of man.

27 They did eat, they drank, they married wives, they were given in marriage, until the day that Noe entered into the ark, and the flood came, and destroyed them all.

28 Likewise also as it was in the days of Lot; they did eat, they drank, they bought, they sold, they planted, they builded;

29 But the same day that Lot went out of Sodom it rained fire and brimstone from heaven and destroyed them all.

30 Even thus shall it be in the day when the Son of man is revealed.

31 In that day, he which shall be upon the housetop, and his stuff in the house, let him not come down to take it away: and he that is in the field, let him likewise not return back.

32 Remember Lot's wife.

God's Sovereign Rule and The Kingdom of Heaven

The earth is the Lord's and the fullness there of, and they that dwell therein. Why would any question God could not be in control? The Scriptures teach His sovereign rule over all? Why then doubt God's sovereignty? The answer is simple the Kingdoms of this present evil age are in rebellion to God, as the world we live in has a system, a governance called the Kingdom of Darkness. Whose chief ruler is the Prince of the Power of the Air, Satan. Does the Kingdom of Darkness then invalidate the sovereign rule of God over the peoples of the earth? Or change God sovereign rule throughout world history, or over the future of the nations? In no way is the sovereign rule of God diminished at the fall of man, as all history, and all humanity will be summoned up in Jesus Christ.

Psalm 24:1-2
24:1-2
1 The earth is the Lord's, and the fulness thereof; the world, and they that dwell therein.

2 For he hath founded it upon the seas and established it upon the floods.

Let us get this right, sin, man's rebellion, Satan, and the Kingdom of Darkness cannot alter God at all. No amount of Gods power or ability was lost. The will of God has not been eliminated by the fall of man. Instead, Jesus Christ has given mankind redemption through His blood. God was not caught off guard as if He did not see of know the future, or see the fall of man, or the rebellion of Satan. The sovereignty of God is not affected by man at all, God determines and then executes His will with no one who has the ability or power to stop Him. Of course, God never acts outside of His character and nature. There is no darkness in Him, changing or corrupting His nature. Our Lord God is omniscient, omnipotent, immutable, no other person, or created being has these characteristics.

Knowing the sovereign rule of God has not diminished with the fall of man, why did Jesus Christ announce the Kingdom of Heaven with His coming? The Kingdom of Heaven then is related to the governance of God among man, as an actual government by man. God had promised this kingdom rule to Abraham, and his progeny. The covenant of the Kingdom was given to Abraham, Isaac, and Jacob but in their lifetimes, they never experienced its establishment on earth. This demonstrates the Kingdom of Heaven requires the resurrection of Abraham, Isaac, and Jacob in order for what God had promised by covenant. Do we realize the Kingdom of Heaven was also promised by covenant to David, and to David's Son, as David would never lack a son to sit on the Throne of David?

Of course, the Kingdom was never established, on earth during the first coming of Jesus Christ. The Roman Empire was never overthrown so the Throne of David, with Jesus Christ as the Son of David ruling from Jerusalem over the nations of the earth was never established at this time. Now we can easily distinguish the Kingdom of Heaven, from the sovereign rule of God. As the Kingdom is an actual kingdom ruled by the Son of David, on the Throne of David, from the New Jerusalem. This puts the literal rule of Jesus Christ as the King over the nations of the earth at the future Second Coming of Jesus Christ. Never in the minds of the original disciples did they think the Kingdom of Heaven was a spiritual kingdom in their hearts, or mystical spiritual because of their new birth, and the presence of the Holy Spirit. Even upon seeing Jesus Christ resurrected from the dead, the original disciples asked if Jesus Christ was going to "restore the Kingdom to Israel," at that time. (Acts 1:6)

The Scriptures are clear, until the Second Coming the Kingdoms of this world (age), will be in rebellion to God, not under the rule of the Kingdom of Heaven. The Kingdom of Heaven is demonstrated to be future by the Scriptures, requires the first resurrection of the saints from the dead, and the physical rule of Jesus Christ on earth. At the Second Coming of the Lord is the Battle of Armageddon where the kings of the earth align themselves with Satan and the Antichrist to fight God. When Jesus Christ returns, He comes as the Lord of Hosts to defeat the armies of the Antichrist, and to set up the Kingdom of Heaven on earth. To set up the Throne of David from the New Jerusalem. It at this time the Kingdoms of this world become the Kingdoms of our God and His Christ.

Revelation 11:15-18
15 And the seventh angel sounded; and there were great voices in heaven, saying, The kingdoms of this world are become the kingdoms of our Lord, and of his Christ; and he shall reign for ever and ever.
16 And the four and twenty elders, which sat before God on their seats, fell upon their faces, and worshipped God,
17 Saying, We give thee thanks, O Lord God Almighty, which art, and wast, and art to come; because thou hast taken to thee thy great power, and hast reigned.
18 And the nations were angry, and thy wrath is come, and the time of the dead, that they should be judged, and that thou shouldest give reward unto thy servants the prophets, and to the saints, and them that fear thy name, small and great; and shouldest destroy them which destroy the earth.
19 And the temple of God was opened in heaven, and there was seen in his temple the ark of his testament:

and there were lightnings, and voices, and thunderings, and an earthquake, and great hail.

Kingdom Now and Christian Nationalism

In the time of Christ, the disciples of the Lord we are looking for the overthrow of Roman government by Jesus Christ. The concept had to do with the Kingdom of Heaven and the rule of Christ as the Son of David. In the Triumphal entry when Jesus Christ rode the colt into Jerusalem many, we are declaring Jesus Christ as King who was taking his rightful position on the throne. The disciples of Jesus Christ were fighting among one another who would be greatest in the Kingdom. Now who would have imagined a week later a Jesus would be dying on the Cross and their dreams of Christ bringing Israel back into worldwide prominence by the Kingdom of Heaven dead. The push to make civil government the kingdom of heaven on earth has always resulted in calamity.

What is the push of modern-day Charismatics? To declare the kingdom of heaven is now by the Church. It has resulted in a false Gospel and false mission. Is the Church responsible for the current national divide we see in politics? Absolutely yes. The church has equated the kingdom of heaven with American government by men who have redefined the Gospel of the Kingdom. The concept has come by a philosophy which teaches the church will cleanse the 7 pillars of culture making for a Christian government. In this way the Kingdom of heaven is now by the church and is being spread all over the world. This philosophy is entirely false based upon presumptions which are entirely manmade. A false Gospel which has divided the body of Christ into choosing political parties. Exalting the President into an unnatural position which God has never intended. As the President goes so does the Christian faith and the kingdom of heaven in America. Here in lies a great deception placing the kingdom of Heaven on earth inside American politics.

The Kingdom of Heaven was never established in the days of Jesus Christ on earth. Neither has it been established in the two thousand years since the Resurrection of Jesus Christ. The fact is the kingdom of Heaven is not brought about by human efforts. All this kingdom building by Church politics has brought a great snare upon the Christian faith and the testimony of American Christians. A man-made kingdom could never bring the rule of Christ into the nations or establish the government of God on the earth. The kingdom now apostles of the New Apostolic Reformation are partly responsible for this false Gospel. Men who took the 7 Mountain Gospel of Kingdom Now and seduced the Church to fight a political battle which has divided the nation and Church. Christians who believe modern day apostles and prophets will establish the true government of the Church and spread the kingdom of heaven by this government all over the world before Jesus Christ returns.

Here is the challenge. The Kingdom of heaven is future at the Second Coming of Jesus Christ. There exists no reality of the Kingdom of Heaven on earth when Jesus Christ is not physically present as the King of the Kingdom. Its Christs physical presence ruling from the New Jerusalem on earth which determines the presence of the Kingdom of heaven. If Christ as King is not present neither is the Kingdom of Heaven. Not getting right the order and time of the Kingdom of heaven in its actual presence and rule has caused the ruin of many who are chasing after a dangling carrot of falsehoods. Let us get this straight, no man, no Church, no government, no nation has ever been able to establish the kingdom of heaven on earth in almost two thousand years. No modern-day apostles and prophets are establishing the kingdom of heaven on earth by church government either.

Simply put, the Kingdom of Heaven is brought by Jesus Christ alone at the Second Coming of the Lord. Until then kingdoms of this present age are hostile to Jesus Christ and the Christian faith. Many Christians are deceived by a false Gospel, and so are all they whom follow the Kingdom Now 7 Mountain Mandate.
Revelation 11:14-19
14 The second woe is past; and, behold, the third woe cometh quickly.

15 And the seventh angel sounded; and there
were great voices in heaven, saying, The kingdoms of
this world are become the kingdoms of our Lord, and of
his Christ; and he shall reign for ever and ever.
16 And the four and twenty elders, which
sat before God on their seats, fell upon their faces, and
worshipped God,
17 Saying, We give thee thanks, O
Lord God Almighty, which art, and wast, and art to
come; because thou hast taken to
thee thy great power, and hast reigned.
18 And the nations were angry, and thy wrath is
come, and the time of the dead, that they should be
judged, and that thou shouldest give reward unto
thy servants the prophets, and to the saints, and them
that fear thy name, small and great; and shouldest
destroy them which destroy the earth.
19 And the temple of God was
opened in heaven, and there was seen in his temple the
ark of his testament: and there
were lightnings, and voices, and thunderings, and an
earthquake, and great hail.

Matthew 7:13-14
13 Enter ye in at the strait gate: for wide is the
gate, and broad is the way, that
leadeth to destruction, and many there be which go
in thereat:
14 Because strait is the gate, and narrow is the

way, which leadeth unto life, and few there be that find it.

Militant Christianity

In so many ways the Kingdom Now Charismatic false Gospel has corrupted the truth faith. Even now after the failed Trump reelection some Charismatics have displayed an increasing aggression against the current government. A language has evolved in some Charismatic circles that a civil war will arise, and Charismatics are being encouraged to take up arms. History has proven whenever the Church declared war it was the result of great corruption. Take for example the Catholic Holy wars, and the Inquisitions where the supposed "kingdom of Heaven" was to fight actual wars in "defense of the Kingdom." The Catholic Church was corrupt to the core wanting to rule over all the nations by religious suppression, and corrupted Federal government.

Even when Christians left England in search or religious freedom the intent was never to make war with England. In Americas Civil War battles were often fought with one Christian General from the South fighting against a Christian General from the North. American Christians were engaged in both the Revolutionary War, and the Civil War. Have you considered the deep corruption which exists inside the Church when brothers in Christ must rise against other brothers in Christ and shed their blood? Never has war been about man's ability to save the world. Of course, throughout all human history of thousands of years, only a little over two hundred years exist where no war or wars were being fought during all those years. War is one of the deepest expressions of human corruption, even though some wars are fought to defend the world against the rise of great evil.

Asking Christians to take up arms in defense of corrupted Government at this time in America is a dangerous position. Take for example Rome's domination of Israel during the times of Jesus Christ, and the original apostles. Jesus Christ said before Pilot the Government, if His Kingdom were of this world then His subjects would come and fight in defense of the King, and Kingdom. However, the Kingdom of Heaven was not to be established at that time. Jesus Christ said His Kingdom was not of this present evil age. Neither has the Kingdom of heaven come by the Church. War in this age will never establish the Kingdom of heaven on earth by the Church. Neither will it bring in the righteousness of God, only men are saved by the new birth are then made the righteousness of God in Christ. The worlds systems will continue in the deep corruption and rebellion to God, but God is calling out men from every nation into the Holy nation of those separated unto Jesus Christ.

In this age it is the Cross and suffering injustice in the name of Jesus Christ. The disciple of Jesus Christ must deny himself and pick up the Cross and fellowship in the sufferings of Jesus Christ. For the first two hundred years of the Christian faith, we see Christians going to lions' dens, to die by the hands of gladiators, to be set on fire as human torches, and too die by crucifixion. Never do we see Jesus Christ, or the original apostles teach the Church to take up arms and go to war with the evil Roman Empire. It was not until the formation of the unholy Roman Catholic Empire armies were constructed in the name of Christianity and in defense of the Catholic Empire called the Kingdom of God.

If Christians in America take up arms over Americas political divide it will be the result of a great evil and gross darkness both in the nation, and the Church. It will be a deep violation of the basic tenants of the Sermon On the Mount where the disciples of Christ are taught the meek will inherit the earth. Blessed are the peace makers who follow Jesus Christ who seek for a coming Kingdom age, for those men will be celebrated as the Sons of God blessed with the right to rule with Jesus Christ in the coming Kingdom of heaven age.

Yes, there will come a war to end all wars, but its origin is out of heaven with Jesus Christ as the Captain of the Hosts, immortal Christians, and Saints of Old, and Gods Holy angels. The final battle of this present evil age is finally a holy righteous war called the Battle of Armageddon. After this battle, the nations will beat their swords into plow shears, and the nations will learn war no more.

Isaiah 2:4
And he shall judge among the nations, and shall rebuke many people: and they shall beat their swords into plowshares, and their spears into pruninghooks: nation shall not lift up sword against nation, neither shall they learn war anymore.

Church Is Not Kingdom of Heaven

It might be interesting for many Christians who have been taught the Church and the Kingdom of Heaven are the same, the Scriptures do not support this philosophy. First of all, the Kingdom has predated the formation of the Church. Second the Church is never called the Kingdom of Heaven in Scriptures. Instead, Christians are to enter the Kingdom after their born-again experience. Third, not everyone born of the Holy Spirit will be qualified to enter the Kingdom of heaven.

Matthew 25:34
[34] Then shall the King say unto them on his right hand, Come, ye blessed of my Father, inherit the kingdom prepared for you from the foundation of the world:

The Church by its very definition is a broader company of believers, while the Kingdom of heaven by its definition is a smaller more restrictive category of believers. The Church Universal is called the Body of Christ and is everyone born of the Holy Spirit saved by the Blood Sacrifice of Jesus Christ. The Kingdom of heaven includes many members of the Body Christ but not every member as some are disqualified from entering the Kingdom of Heaven at the Second Coming of Jesus Christ. Technically speaking, the Kingdom of Heaven will come at the Second Coming of Jesus Christ when at the time Christ transforms the Kingdoms of this present evil age into the Kingdoms of our God and His Christ. The time when the transformation of the worlds Kingdoms happens is after the Great Tribulation, and after the first resurrection of the righteous dead.

Matthew 7:21-23
[21] Not everyone that saith unto me, Lord, Lord, shall enter into the kingdom of heaven; but he that doeth the will of my Father which is in heaven.
[22] Many will say to me in that day, Lord, Lord, have we not prophesied in thy name? and in thy name have cast out devils? and in thy name done many wonderful works?
[23] And then will I profess unto them, I never knew you: depart from me, ye that work iniquity.

Revelation 11:15
[15] And the seventh angel sounded; and there were great voices in heaven, saying, The kingdoms of this world are

become the kingdoms of our Lord, and of his Christ; and he shall reign for ever and ever.

Entrance Into the Kingdom of heaven is at the end of this age and is by qualification at the Judgement Seat of Christ. Not everyone who says Lord, Lord will enter the Kingdom of Heaven, but only they which have done the will of the Father God.

The Parables of the Talents, Pounds, and 10 Virgins all demonstrate some Christians are able to enter the Kingdom age, while others have the door of entrance closed to them. The basis of entrance will be based upon works of faith rewarded at the Judgement Seat of Christ. All works of wood, hay, and stubble are burnt up and have no reward.

The final point is this. The Church is never commanded to build the Kingdom of Heaven on Earth. Neither has the Church been commanded to spread the Kingdom of heaven all over the world before Jesus Christ can return. As popular as these philosophies have become in modern day Charismatic circles, they are a completely false mission. First of all, Jesus Christ builds the Church, and the brings the Kingdom with Him at the Second Coming. Second, the Great Commission is to preach the Gospel making disciples of all nations. Not making fallen nations into the Kingdom of heaven on earth. Notice in almost 2000 years of Church history there has never been a Christian city or nation which has become the Kingdom of Heaven on earth.

Matthew 25:1-2

Then shall the kingdom of heaven be likened unto ten virgins, which took their lamps, and went forth to meet the bridegroom. [2] And five of them were wise, and five were foolish.

Matthew 25:14-15

[14] For the kingdom of heaven is as a man travelling into a far country, who called his own servants, and delivered unto them his goods.
[15] And unto one he gave five talents, to another two, and to another one; to every man according to his several ability; and straightway took his journey.

Luke 19:11-15

[11] And as they heard these things, he added and spake a parable, because he was nigh to Jerusalem, and because they thought that the kingdom of God should immediately appear.   [12] He said therefore, A certain nobleman went into a far country to receive for himself a kingdom, and to return.
[13] And he called his ten servants, and delivered them ten pounds, and said unto them, Occupy till I come.
[14] But his citizens hated him, and sent a message after him, saying, We will not have this man to reign over us.

¹⁵ And it came to pass, that when he was returned, having received the kingdom, then he commanded these servants to be called unto him, to whom he had given the money, that he might know how much every man had gained by trading.

Chapter Eight
Heavenly Treasure and Rewards

Matthew 6:19-24

¹⁹ Lay not up for yourselves treasures upon earth, where moth and rust doth corrupt, and where thieves break through and steal:²⁰ But lay up for yourselves treasures in heaven, where neither moth nor rust doth corrupt, and where thieves do not break through nor steal
²¹ For where your treasure is, there will your heart be also.
²² The light of the body is the eye: if therefore thine eye be single, thy whole body shall be full of light
²³ But if thine eye be evil, thy whole body shall be full of darkness. If therefore the light that is in thee be darkness, how great is that darkness!
²⁴ No man can serve two masters: for either he will hate the one and love the other; or else he will hold to the one and despise the other. Ye cannot serve God and mammon.

The fallen world is full of idols which seek to defile the Church. Perhaps no greater evil comes from the world's mammon. As the Scriptures warn the love of money is the root of all evil, which while some have coveted after having errored from the faith and pierced themselves through with many sorrows. (1 Timothy 6:10)

The power of evil in mammon worship is warned about in the Sermon On the Mount. Here is the break down verse by verse concerning mammon worship:

Verse 19 "Lay not for yourself treasures upon the earth". Now just think the amount of time those who call themselves Christians do this very thing. They spend all their time seeking the things of this world and give Jesus a few hours on Sunday morning.

These worldly goods are corrupted by moths and rust, meaning those worldly goods were kept in store and not used in service to the Lord. In the end the world will consume its own through lies, and theft.

Verse 20: "But lay for yourselves treasures in heaven..." In this way your life as a disciple of Christ is expended in service to Jesus Christ. In contrast taking your earthly treasures in service to the Lord provides you with eternal riches and rewards. Where moths and rust cannot corrupt your treasure, neither can thieves enter to steal. The warning is in seeking worldly treasure you expend your life for treasures which are temporal. In the storing of the worlds treasures is your reward now, and the forfeiture of eternal rewards when earthly treasure is not given in service of Jesus Christ. Treasures laid up in heaven are for future rewards and glory. Treasures which are eternal in nature, with eternal rewards which cannot be corrupted or stolen The challenge to the disciples comes in laying up treasures now in heaven and not using the worlds good now for self.

Verse 21" For where your treasure is, there your heart will be also." Here is a significant fact which cannot be altered. When you give your heart to the treasures of the world you will expend your life in service for them. When your heart is given to the Lord, you can place your treasures in heaven, and not love the things of the world. Your hearts devotion demonstrates who you serve. For you cannot serve God and mammon.

This division is so clear, it is impossible to violate. Christ then demonstrates the principle of an evil eye. Which is the corruption which comes from the love of money:

Verse 22 The light of the body is the eye, if your eye is single, then your whole body will be full of light." The principle is taught the corruption is mammon has the power to defile and darken the interior life of a disciple. While the disciple who will not compromise with the world's richest will be filled with the light of the world Jesus Christ. However, a disciple who has compromised his devotion to Jesus Christ with the world's richest will have the corruption of loving the world fill his interior life with darkness.

Verse 23" But if your eye be evil, your whole body shall be full of darkness. If the light that is in you is darkness, how great is that darkness."

This verse seems to warn disciples after having been illuminated, compromise with the worlds riches which now has resulted in the peril of a great darkness. The warning from the Lord is disciples who once fellowshipped with the Lord in the light now have their bodies full of darkness. How dangerous are the worlds treasures when the saints compromise with God? Shutting themselves off from walking in the light and walking in the world's darkness. Having an evil eye which has sold his soul in exchange for the world's treasures.

Verse 24" No man can serve two masters. For he will either hate the one or love the other. Or else he will hold to the one and despise the other."

Here is the absolute impossibility, you (any man) cannot serve God and mammon. So many in the modern age Church cannot see their own blindness and nakedness before God. As they say we are rich and in need of nothing. Now Jesus Christ after giving the warning of the love of mammon, gives His disciples directives on how to walk out their salvation in this present evil age.

Verse 25 "Therefore I say unto you, take no thought for your life. What you will eat, or what you shall drink, or for your body what you shall put on..."

Has the Church come to realize the basic necessities of life must be fully put into the care of the Lord? For the entire world is chasing these basic issues of life. How difficult is it for fallen man to see their source and supply as coming from God? For a man's life consists more of than this age and lifetime. So, disciples most see by faith beyond this age, and the temporal things of this age. Is not life more than what we eat and what we drink, or what we will wear. The world is lost to temporal survivals but can never escape death or eternal judgment. Disciples of Christ must live towards eternal judgments and rewards, not letting temporal things consume their lives. Robbing them of devotion to Jesus Christ.

Verse 26 "Behold the fowls of the air." Christ then points out how He has ordered His creation as an example of His care and provision. See how the birds are dependent upon God's willingness to feed them. Birds do not gather or store in barns and are dependent upon Gods daily provision. Are you not much better than the birds? If God can take care of His creation, what about man who is of far greater value than birds.

Verse 27 "Which of you by taking thought can add one cubit unto his stature".

Christ then challenges the prevailing worry associated with the fear of lack. Either God will fulfill His promise in being our source and supply, or you will fall into the anxiety of mistrust. When a man worries over basics of life, will it add anything to his life? No, instead fear will drive him outside the rest and assurance of faith in God.

Verse 28 "And why do you take thought for clothing? Consider the lilies of the field."

Our Lord once again points out how He orders His creation. As Creator of Heaven and Earth Jesus Christ has clothed the earth with the glory of His creative ability. Now if Christ has placed such glory in clothing the earth, a glory which fades away, will He not cloth His disciples even more?

Verse 29 "And yet I say unto you, that even Solomon in all his glory was not arrayed like one of these."

Let us consider this promise from the Lord. Solomon is considered the wealthiest man to have ever lived during his day. So glorious was the Kingdom of Solomon those who saw the Temple marveled at its glory and excellence. Gold, silver, and precious stones were all utilized to cover Solomons Temple, and Solomons garments too. God promises a future glorification for all His disciples which trust His provision in this age. A resurrection glory which will by far excel the glory of Solomon's Temple.

Verse 30 "Wherefore, if God so clothes the grass of the field, which is today, and tomorrow is cast into the oven, shall He not much more cloth you little of faith."

The charge comes from the Lord for those who will not trust Him in this age are to be charged with little faith. The Lords charge of the lack of faith can lead the Church to awaken to examine the consequences of the disciples of Christ not measuring up to these commands. As all who are born again of the Holy Spirit are to be judged by Christ at His Second Comings. Hence come the warnings recorded in Matthew chapter seven of Kingdom entrance disqualification. The mistrust of the Lord's provision will lead many Christians to compromise with the world, and its riches.

Verse 31 "Therefore take no thought". The Sermon On the Mount makes clear the disciples of Christ are to put the Kingdom of heaven first even before following after food, drink, and clothing. Your heart and mind must be settled what Christ has promised, He will perform.

Verse 32 "For all these things do the Gentiles seek…" The world which does not follow the commands of Christ not to live after these things. However, for those born of the Spirit we must trust God knows we have a need of these things. The Disciples must entrust their entire lives into God the Fathers care. Picking up the Cross in self-denial and follow after the Lord as a true disciple of Jesus Christ. Putting first Christs commands in their lives.

Verse 33 "But seek first the Kingdom of God..." putting the Kingdom age to come means walking through this present evil age with a forward view. God's promise is to care for His own as they put the Kingdom future first sacrificing their lives in service to the Lord in this age. For all disciples who walk by faith will experience the promise of Gods provision even when the circumstances seem humanly impossible.

Verse 34 "Therefor take no thought for tomorrow, for tomorrow shall take thought for things of itself. Sufficient unto the day is the evil thereof."

In this present evil age, enough opportunity presents itself to doubt Gods promise of provision. However, all who would be a disciple of Jesus Christ must trust the Lord with their day-to-day provision. Which frees the disciples to seek to serve the Lord putting the Kingdom of Heaven as their future rewards.

Seeking Money or Seeking God

Jesus Christ has a lot to say about the influence of money upon the lives of His disciples. In the Sermon On the Mount Jesus Christ warned of the incredible power of money to draw away His disciples by compromising, putting money before living for God. Jesus Christ called the power of corruption which money can generate an "evil eye." Simply put men have their eyes on the world's treasures, seek after, and live for it. Jesus Christ clearly stated; "you cannot serve God and mammon." The world is defined by the corrupting power of mammon.

Let us see what it means to put God before money. First of all, it will be one of the most difficult decisions you will ever make in your life. The whole world rich or poor puts the pursuit of money before God. The disciple of Jesus Christ must seek first the Kingdom of God, and then God becomes your source and supply. Take no thought for your life, what you shall eat, or what you shall drink, or clothing for your body, for your life consists more of than these things. However, if anyone has ever trusted the Lord for these things knows "the anxiety," of not having those basic things for our comfort and security.

Jesus Christ taught the nations (Gentiles) build their cultures around these things. However, when putting God first, you must trust He knows you have need of all these things. The argument goes like this, God created the birds, they do not sow seeds, plant fields, or gather into barns, "yet your Heavenly Father feeds them." Are you not more valuable than the birds? God wants to give us the knowledge, He has made the provision of our lives, we live for God first, and He will supply our daily needs.

Now in all my years of the Christian faith, I have seen most Christians putting their needs first, and then the will of God for their lives second. What is the problem? Trusting God and completely living for Him as His disciple, and not living for your will instead of His. Would you give up your right to live the career you want, to live completely for Jesus Christ as His disciple? You must admit trusting Jesus Christ as a pilgrim, walking by faith now, not loving the world, not laying up treasures on earth is one of the least obeyed commands in modern Christianity.

Consider how God has clothed the flowers with glory, here today gone tomorrow. Jesus Christ then says Solomon the wealthiest man who existed in the world in his day was not clothed in glory like one of these. What does this mean? Isn't wealth and riches fleeting? Chasing after them is surely a wearisome life, full of anxiety and uncertainty. Wealth is no guarantee with God, laying treasures up here on earth, where rust and moths can corrupt, and thieves can break in and steal. Instead seeking first, the Kingdom of God means putting worldly treasure behind, and laying up treasure in heaven which cannot be corrupted. It means in this life you will suffer loss, the cost of doing God's will for your life "means you must sacrifice everything," and come follow Me.

It will be easier for a "camel to go through the eye of the needle," than for a rich man to "enter the kingdom of heaven." Did you get that? Rich man hold on to their treasures and are in constant management of their wealth. They chose this "world and age to live for," instead of not loving the world or things of the world. They are not on a pilgrimage walking through this present evil age knowing the things of the world are temporal and destined to pass away at the Second Coming of Jesus Christ. At the coming of the Lord, will be a new age, "the Kingdom of Heaven on earth." Those who have picked up the Cross in self-denial to follow the Lord will be awarded with Kingdom age glory. It takes faith in God to deny the worlds riches, to be rewarded then. As the apostle Paul in all his suffering has said, "this light affliction which is but for a moment, works for us a far more exceeding and eternal weight of glory." (2 Corinthians 4:17)

Does the power of mammon make for an evil eye? Just see all the men and women who lead the Church who have sold their souls for wealth, fame, and the worlds measure of success.

Matthew 6:19-34
19 Lay not up for yourselves treasures upon earth, where moth and rust doth corrupt, and where thieves break through and steal:

20 But lay up for yourselves treasures in heaven, where neither moth nor rust doth corrupt, and where thieves do not break through nor steal:

21 For where your treasure is, there will your heart be also.

22 The light of the body is the eye: if therefore thine eye be single; thy whole body shall be full of light.

23 But if thine eye be evil; thy whole body shall be full of darkness. If therefore the light that is in thee be darkness, how great is that darkness!

24 No man can serve two masters: for either he will hate the one and love the other; or else he will hold to the one and despise the other. Ye cannot serve God and mammon.

What Would Happen If Marketing the Church Had To Stop?

First of all, first century Christians did not package and sell the Christian faith as a product to be purchased. They did not "sell healing," or make multimillionaires out of healing ministries. The man at the gate Beautiful heard the apostle Peter say, "silver and gold have I none, but what I have given I thee, in the name of Jesus Christ rise up and walk." Apostle Peter had the most prolific working of miracles, even his shadow could cause paralytics to rise and walk. Did Peter exploit the Church over "miracle power," package and sell miracles as a product? History proves Peter was hung on a Cross upside down deeming himself not worthy to be crucified in the same fashion as the Lord Jesus Christ.

The apostle Paul received more revelation knowledge than any man in the history of the Christianity. Did Paul build a "apostolic network of Churches?" Did Paul pad his pocket by promising the "hidden keys of knowledge," so as to create a following? Did Paul exploit his visions, his heavenly encounters, his encounters with Jesus Christ? Was Paul always boasting in supernatural experiences so as to market the Church, Paul had something "no other Christian had?" Or did Paul, appoint elders of Churches he raised up, and made no claim, no name, no Church organization from which Paul could profit? Was Paul put in prison for hazarding his life, when instead he could have profited from the Church? Was Paul beheaded as a martyr, refusing to compromise with the world a fool for Christ?

Now what is the problem? The first century Church was willing to sell everything they had to give up the world's treasures. The apostles were willing to leave everything to preach the Gospel to hostile people groups, to risk martyrdom. All of the early apostles either were martyred or banished in exile. The was no sense of "laying treasures on earth," to make a profit from the Church. So, what would happen if the Church could no longer make a profit?

First of all, many ministries would quit what they are doing, "as there is no money."
Second entire denominations would disband, as the finances required to run their organizations, to pay for the jobs would not be there. Simply put many things which are accounted for Christianity, which has absorbed Christians into organizations would no longer exist, "no money." The motivation which sustained the system would be gone, the well has run dry, no more finances. Cannot live without money so workers would leave the system to find other jobs.

Next authentic Christian faith would replace organization, dependence upon the Lord , Christians who are willing to serve, to trust the Lord for their finances. The result will look more like a "Christian community," where the "one man show would no longer exist." A gross imbalance of distribution of finances comes with "marketing the Church." Now Christians would move in community, like the early Church caring for one another's needs. No super star apostles would arise to make millions of dollars, no one man could exploit the Church. No TV ministry would "attempt to sell Christian trinkets," for TV ministry would only come from time to time as the Lord led. Instead, the entire Church would mobilize to spread the Gospel, in a grass roots more primitive way. No multimillionaire dollar mega Church buildings, instead homes , small groups, and community. It would obviously have more of an organic, community based, relational effort.

It would be the body of Christ moving in concert, with no super stars, one man shows, instead the members in care for one another. The head of the body, Jesus Christ would direct the members of the body, not organizations, or men with the money. The Church would have to pray to fast, to seek first the Lord. The true apostles would rise up when the "corruption of money," attempted to enter the community of believers. As greed and lust and ambition for power would surely grieve the Holy Spirit and prevent the true move of God.

Offerings would still exist, but not to build a man's ministry. Giving would come from authentic needs, no one man or ministry organization would control the finances. Instead, the Church would entrust men and women who had the character to help govern Church affairs, including the care of widows. Apostles would raise up new Churches by walking by faith and trusting the Lords daily provisions as they went forth into cities and nations. Churches would have a heart to sustain the development of new disciples and new Churches, so from time-to-time offerings would be given from one Church to another Church.

The heart of the Church would be giving and laying down our lives to support the Gospel. Seeking first the

Kingdom would be a necessity, food, clothing, and homes would have to be laid in the care of the Lord. Life would be much more basic, and very dependent on the Lord for our daily bread. No man could make money the reason to obey the Lord, instead simple obedience would require our complete surrender to the will of the Lord. The world would shake with the power and glory of the Lord, as the Holy Spirit would be the source of the Church. The spirit of mammon and worldly success would be considered and abomination. Ananias and Sapphira, would be a constant reminder how Satan wants to fill the hearts of Christians, to use money, and greed to corrupt the Church.

I wonder if the Church of Laodicea wants to even let the Lord back in to the Church. It will cost us all the worlds fame and success, and He will take all our money too.

The Temptation of Getting Your Way

Why do people feel so good when the get their own way? Perhaps it is even a good thing something strongly desired. As compared to evil desires which are bluntly wrong, sinful, harming yourself or others. For Christians getting your own way is a grave danger to your walk of faith. Simply put, your way will likely be conformed to the ways of the world. For all that is in the world is the lust of the flesh, lust of eyes, and the pride of life. So not getting your way means a separation from the things of the world by denying yourself and picking up the Cross fellowshipping in the sufferings of Christ. Why would the typical modern day Christian fail to separate from world and be joined to the Lord, the price of sacrificing your own will and desires.

What is the danger? To think the absence of Gods displeasure is His permission to live for your will and way. The modern Church has taught God's blessing on your life is to have an abundance of things. What would a man give in exchange for his soul? What does it profit a man to gain the whole world and lose his soul? What does the spirit of the age, the worlds system do to a man's soul? It causes him to sell out his conscience and become hardened by sin. As a Christian you must guard over your heart with all diligence for out of the heart comes a man's life. What in the world have you given your heart to? To what things, to what pleasures, to what accomplishments are you living for. Just because you prosper in those things does not mean God has given them, or even blessed them for your life. Getting your own way all the time and living for yourself, and then attending a Church service for a few hours during Sunday does not mean you are living for Jesus Christ. Modern Christian life has presented a most dangerous form of worldly Christianity where Christians are told God wants to serve their life.

Where is the correction and discipline for living a worldly life, having it your way? Does the absence of Gods correction, or even rebuke then give you permission to live a self-willed life? Not at all, the absence of Gods rebuke on your life is a great warning. For those who are truly surrendered to the Lord, reproof and correction are become a way of life. For whom the Lord loves He disciplines and scourges every son who He receives. If you are not being corrected and restrained by the Lord for your self will, any sins, and worldly desires you are not being Fathered by God. What happens if you refuse the correction of the Lord and get your way?

The answer lies in the vast numbers of Christians who are the illegitimate sons and daughters who have it their way. For whom the Lord loves He chastens, even whips every son who receives His Fathering. If you are self-selfish, self-absorbed, self-centered child of God getting you own way spending all your time on your will and desires, you have rejected the discipline of the Lord God will set many things in your path to reprove your life, even great suffering, and loss. The cost of selling your soul for the temporal things of this world will be with great sorrow at the Second Coming of Jesus Christ. Self-spoiled worldly Christians will have lost the right of wearing the Crown and ruling with Christ in the Kingdom age. They have sold their birthright for the temporary pleasures of sin and love this present evil age.

Are you an illegitimate child of God? For if you are without Gods will of correction upon your life, of whom

all are partakers who serve Christ, then you are bastards
not sons. You are like Esau who was first born, the legal
heir to his father's inheritance. The right of the first-
born son who sold his birth right for a single carnal meal
of pleasure. Esau did not value his father's house and
the right to rule the family as the future king and priest.
No man can wear the Crown and obtain the Throne
unless trained by His Father. Many who have sold their
souls to self-will living for the world will see on that day
the great treasure which they have forfeited.

Buying Food In the Last Days

For many portions of the world finding your daily bread
is a conscious effort and a necessity for survival. In
America, the availability of food and its abundance does
not require a daily search. However, when the
Coronavirus shut the nations down, Americans ran for
the groceries in a survival mentality. In some cases, the
exhibition of greed, and panic buying revealed many
Americans feel deeply insecure in times of difficulty.
Does faith in Christ require a different reaction than
those who are fighting with their fears of survival?

What did Coronavirus plague reveal? What is our it first
instinct is towards ourselves or reaching out to God. I
can see seeking God first in the face of any life-
threatening circumstance reveals our trust or mistrust.
Jesus Christ taught the Church to seek first the Kingdom
of Heaven, to put our complete trust and reliance upon
the Lord's provision of daily bread.

Satan tempted Jesus in the wilderness with a lack of food, and hunger with a desire to eat. The test was to work a miracle to use His power and turn stones into bread. Jesus quoted Scripture to defeat the temptation, "man shall not live by bread alone but by every word which proceeds out of the mouth of God." Being hungry, not having enough food is a real test, even life threatening but God's promise is provision. Putting God before our natural desires is a big deal, a real test of our security. Why would Satan use the appetites of body to draw men away from God if it were not effective? In the future the control over the nations will include the food supply, the Antichrist will require a "Mark" to buy and sell. With the Mark the ability to have enough food to eat will be in serious jeopardy. Controlling the masses by controlling the food supply by economic regulation is a true Satanic method. Of course, in order to take the "Mark of the Beast," you must deny Jesus Christ, and worship Satan and the Antichrist. The survival instinct will override the nations trust in God in the time of worldwide Catastrophic events.

Right now, seems like a light issue to most Americans as the expectation of the Coronavirus to come to an end within a matter of months is hoped for. However, to trust God for your life just does not naturally happen overnight. Giving the Lord the right to everything in your life requires a deepening surrender. Putting God first and living first for the Lord is not natural for the flesh as it requires a denial of the self-life and picking up the Cross to follow the Lord. In putting the Lord first, God requires the saints to lay up for themselves treasures in heaven. This means you do not put career before God, your bank account, your residence, your basic necessities like food and clothing. Jesus Christ said consider the birds, as they do not build a great store house, and yet your Heavenly Father feeds them, are you not of more value than the birds? Or consider the flowers how God cloths them, even though they are here today and gone tomorrow. God will cloth us, and feed us as we seek first the Lord, His coming Kingdom, and His way of righteousness. Which is different than the peoples of the nations who know not God.

When the Coronavirus virus first shut down the nations did you find yourself drawing near to the Lord. Did you find yourself in an ever-increasing time of prayer, and fellowship in the Word of God? Did you see God was in control, and as always is your source and supply? When you lost the ability to work and make money did you already know your worked for the Lord and your employment was in God's hands. Did you measure your security by your ability to make money, or know there will be times when the economic systems fail? The nations in distress, plagues ravaging the nations, famines which result from plagues making for no natural means of source and supply. Perhaps this why the Bible says the saints are to pray for their daily bread, as God must supply the need even if He must send the ravens with bread.

Is God more important in your life than the very basic things by which we live? I trust in these days the tests which are shaking the whole earth will grow in frequency and in intensity. It is time for the saints all over the world to abandon themselves to God, seeking first the Kingdom and righteousness. Then all these things (food, clothing, and shelter) will be added by God unto you.

Chapter Nine
Judge Not, That You Be Not Judged

Matthew 7:1-5

1 Judge not, that ye be not judged.
2 For with what judgment ye judge, ye shall be judged: and with what measure ye mete, it shall be measured to you again.
3 And why beholdest thou the mote that is in thy brother's eye, but considerest not the beam that is in thine own eye?
4 Or how wilt thou say to thy brother, Let me pull out the mote out of thine eye; and, behold, a beam is in thine own eye?
5 Thou hypocrite, first cast out the beam out of thine own eye; and then shalt thou see clearly to cast out the mote out of thy brother's eye.

Love of the Brethren Involves Correction

What happens when the Church has fallen to the world's influence and has taken her eyes off the Lord? In these days reproof and correction of deception, is a necessity as warned by the Scriptures. In the last days many shall depart from the faith (apostasy), giving heed to seducing spirits (evil spirits) and doctrines of demons. (Teachings which originate from evil spirits). The Bible does not teach popularity, or success in the eyes of masses people makes a man free from deception. Probably, the greatest evidence of this inside organized Christianity is the historical paganism of the faith which came with the Catholic Church. Now days deceptive teachings run rampant everywhere in both Catholicism and Protestant Denominations. The challenge then comes, if you correct your brother, and they are popular or successful, those who bring the correction are charged with being divisive, an accuser of the brethren, and unloving.

The apostle Paul faced a great deal of deception in the 1st century Church, by false prophets, false apostles, called the Gnostics who were bringing their doctrines of demons into the Christian faith. Paul wrote an extensive number of Scriptures instructing the Church on how to deal with the constant threat of Christians falling into error and deception. Here is some advice Paul gave "brothers in Christ," as heresies bring division to the Unity of the Spirit and the bond of peace. Ironically, those who have created the division are often "accredited as being loving," where their charm and personality have covered the real problem of teaching deception.

Paul's instructions for loving the brethren in the midst of the trials of our faith:
1) Seek Christ, and those things above by setting your affections on things above and not on the earth. Sadly, the worldly pull inside of the modern Church has the eyes of many Christians on things like politics, riches, and worldly success.
2) For you are dead, and your life is hid with Christ in God. Makes you wonder how may really see they are dead to self, and only alive in Christ.
3) When Christ appears (Second Coming), then you appear with Him at that time in glory. Until then you deny yourself by picking up the Cross to follow Jesus.
4) Put to death the members of your body which are upon the earth, sexual immorality of any kind evil affections and lust. These things are just idolatry, a worship of self.
5) The wrath of God comes because of these wicked practices.
6) Put off these worldly ways, anger, wrath, malice, blasphemy, and filthy communication. Watch out when you correct your brother, you are

looking for restoration, repentance, and forgiveness.

7) Lie not one to another, including a cloak of covetousness where ministries are portraying a Godly character, but are in truth using and abusing the Church.

8) But now ye also put off all these, anger, wrath, malice, blasphemy, filthy communication out of your mouth.

9) Put on the New Man, by putting off the Old Man.

10) In Christ there are no worldly distinctions, like political agendas, racial hate, and abuse, special privileges for the wealthy, or special privileges for apostles, prophets for in the faith Christ is all, and in all.

11) When the Church glories in a man, those worldly distinctions are creating an "artificial divide in the body of Christ."

Colossians 3:1-17

1 If ye then be risen with Christ, seek those things which are above, where Christ sitteth on the right hand of God.

2 Set your affection on things above, not on things on the earth.

3 For ye are dead, and your life is hid with Christ in God.

4 When Christ, who is our life, shall appear, then shall ye also appear with him in glory.

5 Mortify therefore your members which are upon the earth; fornication, uncleanness, inordinate affection, evil concupiscence, and covetousness, which is idolatry:

6 For which things' sake the wrath of God cometh on the children of disobedience:

7 In the which ye also walked some time, when ye lived in them.

8 But now ye also put off all these, anger, wrath, malice, blasphemy, filthy communication out of your mouth.

9 Lie not one to another, seeing that ye have put off the old man with his deeds.

10 And have put on the new man, which is renewed in knowledge after the image of him that created him:

11 Where there is neither Greek nor Jew, circumcision nor uncircumcision, Barbarian, Scythian, bond nor free: but Christ is all, and in all.

12 Put on therefore, as the elect of God, holy and beloved, bowels of mercies, kindness, humbleness of mind, meekness, longsuffering.

13 Forbearing one another, and forgiving one another, if any man have a quarrel against any: even as Christ forgave you, so also do ye.

14 And above all these things put on charity, which is the bond of perfectness.

15 And let the peace of God rule in your hearts, to the which also ye are called in one body: and be ye thankful.

16 Let the word of Christ dwell in you richly in all wisdom; teaching and admonishing one another in psalms and hymns and spiritual songs, singing with grace in your hearts to the Lord.

17 And whatsoever ye do in word or deed, do all in the name of the Lord Jesus, giving thanks to God and the Father by him.

The Dogs and Pigs

Matthew 7:6

⁶ Give not that which is holy unto the dogs, neither cast ye your pearls before swine, lest they trample them under their feet, and turn again and rend you.

Right after teaching on judging your brother, especially in hypocrisy the Lord then warns of the dogs and pigs. Obviously, this passage of Scriptures is referring to two different kinds of people. So, judgment is required to help the Disciples of Christ identify certain characteristics of people whom the Lord call dogs and pigs. First of all, never are those who are the Sons of God born of the Holy Spirit referred to as dogs or pigs. So, those who are being judged with those characteristics are men and women who are outside of the Church. Some people have such a character who are not part of the body of Christ and are judged as unclean.

Whom do the Scriptures say are the dogs?

Deuteronomy 23:17-18

¹⁷ There shall be no whore of the daughters of Israel, nor a sodomite of the sons of Israel.

18 Thou shalt not bring the hire of a whore, or the price of a dog, into the house of the LORD thy God for any vow: for even both these are abomination unto the LORD thy God.

Seems according to the law whoredom being practiced as in sodomy, or prostitution could qualify as the uncleanness of dog like character. The price of a dog means the price given to a male prostitute. In sodomy, or female prostitution. One who habitually practices sexual immorality, or sexual perversity, or sexual uncleanness would be considered to possess the unclean nature which could be judged as an unholy dog. This might be offensive to many who say we should not judge another person, but to be tolerant to all. However, the position of Christians not judging is simply not true. We are to expose the hidden things of darkness and reprove those things which are done in secret.

Ephesians 5:5-11

5 For this ye know, that no whoremonger, nor unclean person, nor covetous man, who is an idolater, hath any inheritance in the kingdom of Christ and of God.
6 Let no man deceive you with vain words: for

because of these things cometh the wrath of God upon the children of disobedience.

7 Be not ye therefore partakers with them.

8 For ye were sometimes darkness, but now are ye light in the Lord: walk as children of light:

9 (For the fruit of the Spirit is in all goodness and righteousness and truth;)

10 Proving what is acceptable unto the Lord.

11 And have no fellowship with the unfruitful works of darkness, but rather reprove them.

In the dogs and pigs reference seems Jesus Christ is teaching not to let those worldly influences into the Church which is practiced by the unregenerate. The clean and the unclean were differentiated by the law. Dogs and pigs were both considered unclean animals which could defile the worshiper of God in Israel. The emphasis is dogs are unclean, and unholy and should not be considered part of the Church. It not Christians should not try to reach the sexually immoral, instead they are to be judged under the wrath of God, and unclean until their conversion by salvation in Jesus Christ.

False prophets are also considered dogs. The prophet Isaiah identifies the false prophets in Israel as dumb dogs who cannot bark and warn Israel of coming danger.

Isaiah 56:10-11

[10] His watchmen are blind: they are all ignorant, they are all dumb dogs, they cannot bark; sleeping, lying down, loving to slumber.
[11] Yea, they are greedy dogs which can never have enough, and they are shepherds that cannot understand: they all look to their own way, everyone for his gain, from his quarter.

The significance of false prophets in both the Old and New Testaments is a big part of Scriptures and the Sermon On the Mount. Once again keeping the dogs out of the holy assembly is a big part of judging a man's position before Christ.

Notice how the apostle Peter teaches false teachers, false shepherds, are men who have eyes full of adultery. They are like dogs who return to their own vomit, or pigs who return to wallowing in the mire.

2 Peter 2:22
[22] But it is happened unto them according to the true proverb, The dog is turned to his own vomit again; and the sow that was washed to her wallowing in the mire.

Which leads us into who does Christ refer to as the pigs? Swine as a principle in Scripture is completely unclean. Once again, the power of defilement is being emphasized by a person which is allowed influence into the Church.

Isaiah 66:1-3

Thus, saith the LORD, The heaven is my throne, and the earth is my footstool: where is the house that ye build unto me? and where is the place of my rest? **2** For all those things hath mine hand made, and all those things have been, saith the LORD: but to this man will I look, even to him that is poor and of a contrite spirit, and trembles at my word. **3** He that killeth an ox is as if he slew a man; he that sacrificeth a lamb, as if he cut off a dog's neck; he that offereth an oblation, as if he offered swine's blood; he that burneth incense, as if he blessed an idol. Yea, they have chosen their own ways, and their soul delighteth in their abominations.

In reference to pigs, the Lord might be referencing religious leaders, and even other religions. Bringing pigs' blood into the house of the Lord and sacrificing pigs' blood upon the alter of the Lord is to draw the wrath of God. In our day, the Church must watch mixing the holy things of the Lord with other religions, or other beliefs which are outside the boundary of the Christian faith.

Today that danger exists in the Ecumenical Movement where many religious leaders are attempting to combine the Christian faith with other religions. In the process the Cross of Jesus Christ is compromised. Those leaders will falsely state there are many paths to God, and Christians worship the same God as Islam, or other major religions. Here is why as the Sermon On the Mount continues to teach the commands of Jesus Christ, and the significance of the straight and narrow way is emphasized. Instead of combing the Christian faith with other world religions creating one super worldwide Church of many religions, and religious beliefs. Jesus Christ narrows the way so as to make the commands and doctrines of Jesus Christ the only ones for the Disciples of Jesus Christ to obey.

Do not give what is holy to dogs. For the Disciples of Jesus Christ many things which are given by God are very precious. Often Jesus Christ would more completely reveal the truths of the mysteries of the Kingdom to His disciples behind closed doors after the masses had departed. The Church has been given many sacred and holy things like the Lords Supper and the promise of the coming Marriage

Supper of the Lamb. How those outside the deep counsels of the Lord despise the priceless pearls of the Lord. Often these deep truth come from deep devotion and surrender of a disciple's commitment to Jesus Christ. These are pearls which come from suffering with Christ, just as a pearl in nature is formed by pain inside the shell of claims.

Neither give you pearls to the swine, lest the trample them under their feet. Its like when Christ revealed a precious truth of His true person and identity as the Christ, the Son of God to the religious leaders, and they picked up stones to stone Him. The religious leaders who are outside of Christ will not receive these precious pearls as those who have suffered to obtain them. Instead, will place no value in these Godly pearls of truth, and will trample them under their feet. Is this not a similar warning Christ gave earlier in the Sermon On the Mount when He warned if the Church were to lose its saltiness, it would be cast out by men, and trodden underfoot. Not only trodden underfoot, but the pigs would turn again and tear at you. Is this not the testimony of Jesus Christ on the Cross when the religious leaders of His day mocked and derided Him.

Psalm 22:14-22

14 I am poured out like water, and all my bones are out of joint: my heart is like wax; it is melted in the midst of my bowels.

15 My strength is dried up like a potsherd; and my tongue cleaveth to my jaws; and thou hast brought me into the dust of death.

16 For dogs have compassed me: the assembly of the wicked have inclosed me: they pierced my hands and my feet.

17 I may tell all my bones: they look and stare upon me.

18 They part my garments among them and cast lots upon my vesture.

19 But be not thou far from me, O LORD: O my strength, haste thee to help me.

20 Deliver my soul from the sword, my darling from the power of the dog.

21 Save me from the lion's mouth: for thou hast heard me from the horns of the unicorns.

22 I will declare thy name unto my brethren: in the midst of the congregation will I praise thee.

Chapter Ten
The Narrow Way

Matthew 7:13-14
13 Enter ye in at the strait gate: for wide is the
gate, and broad is the way, that
leadeth to destruction, and many there be which go
in there at:
14 Because strait is the gate, and narrow is the
way, which leadeth unto life, and few there be that
find it.

The Narrow Way

Narrow is the way which leads to life, and few are they
which find it. Are there any more certain words as these
spoken by Jesus Christ? What is more common to man
than a self-centered, self-love, and self-preservation,
way of life? The masses Christian or otherwise will never
find the straight and narrow way. The broadways is the
world's way, it is the self-life, many are the saints who
are born again of the Spirit, but never enter into the
narrow way of picking up the Cross in self-denial. The
most unnatural way of this life is to suffer the loss of all
things, to count all things loss, and to value those things
as dung. Picking up the Cross being crucified to the
world and your self-life. Do we not see how repulsive,
how offensive, how unnatural the crucified life really is?

The context of the passage which Jesus Christ declared the narrow way was the Sermon On the Mount. Is there anything more backwards, more turned upside down life, than the characteristics of what Jesus Christ described true disciples were to live? Love your enemies, bless them which curse you, pray for them which despitefully use you, do good to them which hate you. Do you not see, the Cross of the disciple must sacrifice the world's values? Especially the highest value of all "putting yourself first."

Now many Christian assume because they are born again, this gives them an advantage, God is in the business of promoting their lives. Many simply have taken their lives which were before Christ, and now after coming into saving faith still have failed to surrender their self-life. Christians who have just " put a God label on their selfishness," and call it God's blessing. This kind of Cross less Christianity is dominating modern day pulpits and is the commercial and entertainment world of the Church.

What happens in real life though. This present evil age is in complete contradiction to the walk of faith. The Christian is a stranger and pilgrim on a journey towards the Second Coming, and the Kingdom of Heaven on Earth. The loss must be real in this time, you must redeem the time for the days are evil. The Scriptures inform us not to be surprised at the fiery trails which have come upon our life as if some strange thing were happening to us. "But rejoice," the outcome is you are suffering in Christ's suffering. Losing out now, but when Christ is revealed in glory (Second Coming) you may glad with "exceeding joy."

What is Peter saying, in the walk of faith you must suffer reproach for Christ. Peter is teaching it is God's you will suffer for well doing. God orders your environment to train and discipline you for the next age. Many things which come along in our life causing us to suffer loss, to see the self-life crucified. If you do not have your eyes on the Lord, and the glorification of the saints at the Second Coming, you will take offense.

Many are the offended in Christ, who have stopped walking in the straight and narrow way. They have thought the cost of their personal Cross to be too high a price. They have left of from the Lord to walk in the broad way of a self-centered love and have refused the Cross. The broad way is their course, in which they have their "reward now." Christian, do you understand the narrow way is about the Christian journey, and the trials of our faith, which are God's way of ordering our environment of the Cross? Once you enter the straight gate coming into saving faith in Christ, the way of faith is to fellowship in the sufferings of Christ. The shame, the pain, the loss, the rejection, the aloneness, is a very narrow way indeed.

However, as the apostle Paul has said the in the face of his enormous suffering; " this light affliction is bit for a moment, is working in me an exceedingly eternal weight of glory." Paul had his eyes on the prize of the high calling in Christ, and knew the Cross was before the Throne. Anyone who refuses the Cross in this age, will not be qualified for the next. In this way they face their own demise following the crowds who refuse the fellowship of the Cross. In this way a man is destroyed by his own flesh, and selfish gratification.

1Peter 4:12-19

12 Beloved, think it not strange concerning the fiery trial, which is to try you, as though some strange thing happened unto you:

13 But rejoice, inasmuch as ye are partakers of Christ's sufferings; that, when his glory shall be revealed, ye may be glad also with exceeding joy.

14 If ye be reproached for the name of Christ, happy are ye; for the spirit of glory and of God resteth upon you: on their part he is evil spoken of, but on your part, he is glorified.

15 But let none of you suffer as a murderer, or as a thief, or as an evildoer, or as a busybody in other men's matters.

16 Yet if any man suffer as a Christian, let him not be ashamed; but let him glorify God on this behalf.

17 For the time is come that judgment must begin at the house of God: and if it first begin at us, what shall the end be of them that obey not the gospel of God?

18 And if the righteous scarcely be saved, where shall the ungodly and the sinner appear?

19 Wherefore let them that suffer according to the will of God commit the keeping of their souls to him in well doing, as unto a faithful Creator.

The Gate At the End of Journey

In the Christian faith many place entrance into the Kingdom the Kingdom of heaven at the beginning of one's salvation. However, this belief conflicts with the teaching of Scriptures. The gate into the Kingdom of heaven is described as straight and narrow. Its entrance is proved to be at the Second Coming of the Lord rather than entered upon by one's salvation now. Jesus Christ is clear many will come to Him on the day saying Lord Lord but will not be able to enter through the gate being disqualified from entering into the Kingdom of Heaven. Many will teach those who could not enter were never saved in the first place. Why seek first the Kingdom by a straight and narrow way if all may enter in the beginning? As difficult it is to accept the warning of Kingdom forfeiture, it is given to Christ's disciples not to the unsaved. For how can a man dead in sin serve the Lord, or put seeking the Kingdom first in their lives? Or how can a man call Jesus Christ Lord until first born of the Holy Spirit? Jesus Christ made it clear a man who is dead in sin cannot even see the kingdom of Heaven.

The Kingdom in Scriptures is a future salvation or entrance. It is walk requires a very narrow limited way after coming into saving faith. You must seek to enter into through the narrow gate, as broad is the way to destruction and many are, they who go therein. In this case the destruction is the judgment which will happen to Christians at the Judgment Seat of Christ. Salvation in this case is not of one's forgiveness's of sins as the Cross has already provided this through the blood of Jesus Christ. Instead of judging our eternal life, the judgment Seat of Christ judges our fitness for qualification in ruling with Jesus in the Kingdom of Heaven age. That is why not everyone who says Lord Lord will enter through the straight and narrow way into the Kingdom of Heaven. Not a loss of eternal life, instead a loss of entrance into the Kingdom age.

Why won't the Lord open the door of entrance into the Kingdom to many of His own? They profess an intimate knowledge of the Lord, while Christ professes them as workers of iniquity. Jesus says for them to depart for He never knew them in the way they profess themselves before the Lord. Here is a warning, prophecy did not save them, neither working of miracles. So many modern Charismatic teachers say signs and wonders are evidence of the Kingdom, but Jesus Christ did not allow entrance into the Kingdom on the basis of miracles. You can give prophecies and work miracles and still be disqualified from entering into the Kingdom of Heaven age.

What are the qualification for Kingdom of Heaven entrance?

Blessed are the poor in spirit for theirs is the kingdom of heaven. Blessed are the meek for they are the ones who inherit at the end of this present evil age. They are the true workers of the Lord who must suffer injustice and forgive those who despitefully use them. You can see why the peacemakers are the true inheritors of the kingdom, as they must suffer great loss in this age to qualify for the next age. Hardly can a man take the Cross now, to be crowned in the next age then. The Cross is the straight and narrow way, and few are they which find it. This is the way to entrance into the Kingdom and not many are willing to walk this way to be crowned with the right to rule and reign with Jesus Christ in the next age.

Remember you must forgive, or you will not qualify for the Kingdom. To be angry, hateful, and unforgiving of your brother's offense will cause many to forfeit their future inheritance into the kingdom age. You hold onto your brothers' sin, while Jesus Christ died for your sin. What a vital authentic forgiveness really is. It is matter of entrance or exclusion.

Without Holiness No Man Shall See God

Hebrews 12:14
14 Follow peace with all men, and holiness, without which no man shall see the Lord:

This Scripture is very troubling as it is written to Christians in the context of accepting or rejecting God's discipline. Those saints who reject the discipline of the Lord are considered illegitimate sons. Can a Christian be born again, and still be rejected by God on the basis of unholy living? The answer is yes, but the debate usually runs along the lines of losing your salvation or not. So, the not seeing God, would be the loss of eternal life to some. However, the context seems to be a son given birth right by being the first born of the family but refusing the fathers training for the family inheritance. In this case it would be the forfeiture of the right of the first-born son.

To prove the point, the sentence is followed by the life of Esau. Who is the first born of Isaac, but sold his birth right to his brother Jacob for a bowl of lintels? The contrast being Esau despised his birthright, made light of the father's family Inheritance, while Jacob wrestled with God and man to have the rights of the first born. The Scriptures demonstrate a child born of the father can lose the right of the first-born son by unholy living but is still considered part of the family. Esau did this very thing, living an immoral life considered the birth right of Gods inheritance a light thing. Esau was a fornicator who followed after the worlds immoral state, while Jacob considered the right of the first born what to live for.

The Scriptures says an immoral son who will not receive the fathers training and discipline will not see God. In this case not seeing God means Esau, lost the right of inheritance, and was disinherited from the fathers blessing. When it came to for the father to recognize the right of the first-born son, Esau was rejected disqualified by a life of unholy living. Even though Esau repented at the time of the blessing, Esau being in tears, the right of the first born was placed upon Jacob instead. "Will not see God," means rejected from the coming inheritance of God. Isn't this the same warning the apostle Paul gives Christians who are living unholy lives after being born again?

Paul warns born again Christians of losing the rights of the family inheritance by disqualification, unholy living. In this case the inheritance of the first-born sons is called the Kingdom of heaven. As you can see in the Book of Hebrews, are warnings given to Christians not to have an evil heart of unbelief in departing from the Lord. The comparison is to sinful Israel who was delivered by the "Passover Blood of the Lamb," but failed to enter into their Promised Land at the end of their journey. The reason their bodies fell in the wilderness outside of the promised inheritance, was the result of sin. These blood bought children of God rebelled against God's direction and correction. So, it is with many Christians who live after the flesh after being born again.

These saints who like sinful Israel will disqualify
themselves from the right of the first-born son, and the
future entrance into the kingdom of heaven at the end
of the age. That is why Jesus Christ also warned of
failure to enter into the Kingdom age with saints who
fail in obedience. "Not everyone who says to Me Lord,
Lord shall enter the Kingdom of Heaven...depart from
Me you that work iniquity." I never knew you means I
do not recognize your works as righteous and will not
recognize you for kingdom of heaven entrance. The
kingdom age is the reward for all the saints who lived
separated righteous holy lives during their lifetimes.
Jacob did during his lifetime, Esau did not. Enter the
Kingdom age through the straight and narrow way for
few are they who will separate unto God receiving the
full training and discipline which qualify them for the
right of first-born sons. The right to rule and reign with
Jesus Christ as immortal king priests in the next age.

Matthew 7:21-23
21 Not everyone that saith unto me, Lord, Lord, shall
enter into the kingdom of heaven; but he that doeth the
will of my Father which is in heaven.
22 Many will say to me in that day, Lord, Lord, have we
not prophesied in thy name? and in thy name have cast
out devils? and in thy name done many wonderful
works?
23 And then will I profess unto them, I never knew you:
depart from me, ye that work iniquity.

Hebrews 12:14-17

14 Follow peace with all men, and holiness, without which no man shall see the Lord:

15 Looking diligently lest any man fail of the grace of God; lest any root of bitterness springing up trouble you, and thereby many be defiled.

16 Lest there be any fornicator, or profane person, as Esau, who for one morsel of meat sold his birthright.

17 For ye know how that afterward, when he would have inherited the blessing, he was rejected: for he found no place of repentance, though he sought it carefully with tears.

Galatians 5:13-21

13 For, brethren, ye have been called unto liberty; only use not liberty for an occasion to the flesh, but by love serve one another.

14 For all the law is fulfilled in one word, even in this; Thou shalt love thy neighbour as thyself.

15 But if ye bite and devour one another, take heed that ye be not consumed one of another.

16 This I say then, Walk in the Spirit, and ye shall not fulfil the lust of the flesh.

17 For the flesh lusteth against the Spirit, and the Spirit against the flesh: and these are contrary the one to the other: so that ye cannot do the things that ye would.

18 But if ye be led of the Spirit, ye are not under the law.

19 Now the works of the flesh are manifest, which are these, Adultery, fornication, uncleanness, lasciviousness,
20 Idolatry, witchcraft, hatred, variance, emulations, wrath, strife, seditions, heresies,
 21 Envyings, murders, drunkenness, revellings, and such like: of the which I tell you before, as I have also told you in time past, that they which do such things shall not inherit the kingdom of God.

A Christ Centered Life

Within the ranks of men and women who are born again is the struggle to live a truly Christ centered life. Simply put a Christ centered life is where a born-again Christian has surrendered fully to the will of God for their life. It simply means that Jesus Christ comes first in living, the child of God has picked up the Cross to fully follow Jesus Christ, in denying themselves as a true disciple of Jesus Christ. Now after coming into saving faith many things will arise to prevent the Christ centered life, the most common being personal sin. The many things' Christians can do which violate the commandments, which transgress against the commands of Jesus Christ.

In the life of Christians is the difficulty of denying the works of the flesh. Those temptations and desires which come from the sin nature, but those who are Christ's have crucified those lusts, passions, and desires. The body of sin which once dominated the born-again Christian was "crucified with Christ," so the bondage to sin, the old man was put to death. A born-again child of God is no longer a slave to sin. However, the sinful passions and desires are still present in our flesh, as the result a Christian can walk in the flesh, and not in the Spirit. Now the mind set on the flesh is a great problem in the lives of Christians, so there is a battle with crucifying the flesh with its sinful desires. Some habits of the flesh can hinder your progress in the Lord for a very long time. Just when you think you have put away those old sinful habits of the flesh, they can crop up again with "new force." So, the battle with an up again, down again roller coaster ride with sin and the flesh can become a common experience inside the Christian walk of faith. No person who is born again can say they have no sin, or does not struggle with temptation, as the flesh is an ever-constant part of Christians learning to overcome.

Now for those who have grown in grace accepting the discipline of the Lord, the flesh has been severally dealt with. The Cross has been applied to many seasons of growth and maturation, where suffering in surrender of fleshly desires has been a real battle. For those who denied themselves putting the Cross of Jesus into their lives, and who have accepted the discipline of God the Father have been chastised by God's disciple. Now no discipline seems joyful but sorrowful for the moment, but in accepting the correction God's discipline will develop the peaceable fruit of righteousness (right living). You can often see the results of Gods children who are under the discipline of the Lord, as they are saddened by their flesh, and longing for real freedom from fleshly sin and desires.

The crucified life is the Christ centered life and is the result of Christian growth and maturation. A man who has surrendered completely to the Lord in a Christ centered life is no longer their own, their life is now Christ. Their affections and desires have been deeply dealt with, so now their desire is solely for Jesus Christ, and Gods will for their life. In truth a Christ centered person has been crucified to the world, and the world has been crucified to them. Things which use to have such "pull, attention, affection, thoughts, and desires," have been put into the Cross in a surrendered submitted will to God. This man Is truly grown in grace and is become a mature follower of Jesus Christ, what the Scriptures identify as a Spiritual man. Accompanying the life of a Christ centered spiritual man is the wisdom of God, they ability to "discern the things of the Spirit." This Christ centered person is able to discern the leading of the Holy Spirit and recognizes demonic counterfeits and imitation.

The natural man on the other hand is still bound up by the carnal nature and cannot discern the things of the Spirit. The carnal man cannot yet rightly divide the Word of God, comparing spiritual things, by the Spirit.

This is the state of the modern Church, men and women who have yet to be deeply affected by a life of surrender. Putting their own will and desires into the things of world creating great mixture. Also, today the Church has received many demonic counterfeits as "the presence of God, or the Holy Spirit," because the carnal desires of Christians. In reality an imitation of God where Christians are being seduced by evil spirits. So much of what is put off as the supernatural from God, is simply evil spirits playing off the unrenewed minds of carnal Christians with sensuous mystical lying visions, and "angels of light."

The carnal Church loves spiritual experiences, and cares not to test the spirits to see where their supernatural encounters come from. A spiritual man is not seduced by spiritual experiences, and only wants the life of Christ so is not to draw away from the Lord giving place to demonic counterfeits and seduction. It is time for the Charismatic Church to admit her immaturity and lack of discernment. To stop glorying in leaders who cannot discern the things of the Spirit. Who are teaching doctrines of demons, and will not grow up the body of Christ into a spiritual mature man? The fullness of the measure of the stature which belongs to Christ.

The Golden Rule
Matthew 7:7-12
7 Ask, and it shall be given you; seek, and ye shall find; knock, and it shall be opened unto you:

8 For every one that asketh receiveth; and he that
seeketh findeth; and to him that knocketh it shall be
opened.
9 Or what man is
there of you, whom if his son ask bread, will he
give him a stone?
10 Or if he ask a fish, will he give him a serpent?
11 If ye then, being evil, know how to
give good gifts unto your children, how
much more shall your Father which
is in heaven give good things to them that ask him?
12 Therefore all things whatsoever ye
would that men should do to you, do ye even so to
them: for this is the law and the prophets.

The Golden Rule of grace then, which conveys in full the
teaching of our Lord in the Sermon on the Mount, is "
the narrow gate." On another occasion he compared
the severity of His requirements with a needle's eye,
and the inability of the rich man to comply, with the
impossibility of a camel's passing through the narrow
opening. Yet that is the way to the kingdom of heaven.
Jesus' doctrine in the Sermon on the Mount must be
received by us, in order to enter through the gate on
the way.
" Tho way " is the practice which results from the
reception of our Lord's peculiar precepts. The gate
decides the way. The way begins from the gate and
streams from it up to tho goal, which is either " life," or
" destruction." There is no walking in, the way, save by

entrance at tho gate. A life in accordance with Christ's commands can only spring from acknow- ledgment of His authority ns a teacher. Hence Christianity is several times in tho Acts called " the way." Saul desired " letters to Damascus, to the synagogues, that if ho found any of the way [Greek], whether men or women, he might bring them bound unto Jerusalem : " Acts ix. 2. " But when certain
persons were hardened, and spake evil of the way before the multitude, he departed from them." " Now about that timo there arose no small stir about the way : " Acts xix. 9, 23 ; xxii. 4 ; xxiv. 22.
Sermon On the Mount Expounded pg. 296 Robert Govett

Perhaps by this time readers of the Sermon On the Mount can see the absolute impossibility of fulling Christs commands in the Sermon without a complete dependence on God. After accounting the difficulty of the straight and narrow way, Christ once again reminds His disciples of Gods provision along the way. Jesus Christ teaches His disciples to seek from God the Father those things which are necessary to walk out the Sermons Golden Rule. " Therefore all
things whatsoever ye would that men should do to you, do ye even so to them: for this is the law and the prophets."

The demands of loving not only our brethren, but our enemies also has brought the Disciples of Jesus Christ to the straight and narrow way. As the masses of this present evil age would never make it their condition in life to love their enemies. The disciples must seek God the Father for the strength and provision to obey these difficult love commandments. In asking God our Father we acknowledge we receive His grace and provision. Despite any of our inability, the Father will hear our earnest prayers, as we seek Him, we will find. As we knock up heaven's door in prayer, our Fathers provision is opened unto us.

Now because of the difficulty of the straight and narrow way, one might doubt the goodness of God the Father. Jesus Christ does a comparison with earthly fathers who being evil in comparison God the Father and His unfailing love. What father would not give their own children what is necessary? Would a father deny his own son the daily bread which would sustain his life? In the son who asks his earthy father for bread, would his own father supply him a stone instead? Or if a son were to ask for a fish in hunger, would a loving father hurt his own flesh and blood and give a serpent instead? Jesus Christ points out the nature of earthly fathers is to care for their sons, so then how much more would our heavenly Father give those good things to those disciples who ask of Him? Of course, the context is for those who are Christs disciples seeking to walk in the straight and narrow way of the love commands in the Sermon On the Mount.

Now for the teaching of Christs golden rule.
"Therefore allthings whatsoever yewould that men shou
ld do to you, do ye even so to them: for this is the
law and the prophets." The point being in obeying the
love commands in the Sermon On the Mount, even
when men are your enemies, you are to do with them
the same way you would desire to be treated. The
summation of the love commands is to treat those with
grace and mercy, the same way you would have the
Lord judge and forgive you. The Ten Commandments
teach to love the Lord our God with all our life, and to
love our neighbor as ourselves. In this way the Golden
Rule of the Sermon On the Mount is the fulfillment of
the Law and the Prophets.

Chapter Eleven
The Peril of the False Prophets

Matthew 7:15-20
[15] Beware of false prophets, which come to you in
sheep's clothing, but inwardly they are ravening wolves.
[16] Ye shall know them by their fruits. Do men gather
grapes of thorns, or figs of thistles?

[17] Even so every good tree bringeth forth good fruit; but
a corrupt tree bringeth forth evil fruit.
[18] A good tree cannot bring forth evil fruit, neither can a
corrupt tree bring forth good fruit.
[19] Every tree that bringeth not forth good fruit is hewn

down and cast into the fire.

[20] Wherefore by their fruits ye shall know them.

Judging the Prophets

What is a true New Testament Prophet? In the Charismatic Movement this question needs great clarification and accountability. Are there any prophets today which are of the stature of an Old Testament prophet like Elijah, Jeremiah, or John the Baptist? The answer is clearly no, as no New Testament prophet speaks the infallible word of the Lord. The message given New Testament prophets has already been given to them and are recorded in the Scriptures as the doctrines of Jesus Christ. You will see no New Testament prophets bringing in their own private interpretations of prophecy. It is forbidden as even the New Testament apostles were taught the doctrines of Jesus Christ. Apostle Paul clearly acknowledges he was taught the Gospel by Christ Himself. Also, anyone who teaches or preaches another Gospel is accursed by God. Do not let anyone go beyond what has already been established in the Scriptures. Also, do not let anyone who calls themselves an apostle or prophet say they have been given new light of revelation on old warn out interpretations of Scriptures. You are in danger of following a false prophet and heretic.

The true prophets preach the Cross, Jesus Christ and His crucifixion. True prophets have a passion to impart the knowledge of Christ through giving the saints the meat of Gods written word. Their primary mission is to develop the saints into the fulness of the stature which belongs to Christ. They come forth with sound doctrines which cause the saints to grow up into Him, which is Christ, the head of the Church, the body of Christ. That we be no longer children tossed to and fro by every wind of doctrine, and the cunningness of man. Which means the true prophets have real discernment knowing the difference between the authentic and imitation. Which leads us to one of the major issues in modern day prophets and prophetic ministry. The false prophetic cannot discern between dreams and visions which are from God, and those which come from evil spirits. Much of what is said by the prophets came from a dream, or a vision, or an angel is in fact evil spirits imitating the things of God. A New Testament Prophet must know when revelations and spiritual experiences are not from God.

The restraint a prophet must have, self-control a fruit of the Spirit is a must when being pressured to give a word of prophecy. Modern prophets are being compelled to tell everyone they are around the prophetic experiences they are having or pushed to give a word of prophecy. If you are being pushed all the time to predict, or prophesy you are being manipulated by the flesh and evil spirits. The spirit of the prophets are subject to the prophets. You are not being pushed or forced by God, or by angels, or by dreams or visions. All this open heavens anything goes has created a false prophetic ministry with angels of light, and familiar spirits of the occult which are being passed along as the Spirit of God. Let us be straight forward, anyone who says they are a prophet and teaches on portals into heaven, or astral travel in the spirit is operating in occult counterfeits. In true prophetic ministry you cannot direct or guide visions, or angels, or encounters upon demand. You are functioning in a false Holy Spirit and are being deceived by evil spirits. Only God determines who and when a true vision, dream or angelic encounter will happen. No prophet, apostle, or Christian mystic can play Holy Spirit.

This rule is steadfast and without exceptions and has become the primary reason so many false predictions and false prophetic manifests today. If you are a New Testament prophet, you are not guiding and directing the Church. Your prophetic predictions are futile as the Holy Spirit has been given to every born-again child of God. For as many are led of the Spirit these are the Sons of God. Your Presidential predictions are cannon fodder, they mean nothing, and are only sensational. What has been the recent failures of many so-called Trump prophets? They are trying to direct the Church through false predictions which are based upon a false Gospel. Trump Prophets believe God has exalted President Trump as a modern-day Cyrus as a savior of the nation. No man has been given that position or responsibility, as corruption deep in the state is in the hearts of those are lost in sin. Christian government is not possible in a fallen world whose Prince is the Power of the Air. Satan and the kingdom of darkness have been given authority in the nations to deceive, and government is one of their primary ways of corruption. Only the Cross of Jesus Christ can deliver men from the Kingdom of Darkness, that is why the false prophets falsely predict a Christian government will save the nation. They falsely predicted Trump would be the person to lead the Christian government into a great international revival. Every time the Trump prophets attempt to predict this manmade philosophical belief they were prophesying against the Scriptures.

To discern the prophets as false is easy as they invalidate what has already been written. They keep attempting to direct the Church into a false mission by using prophetic predictions against the authority of Scriptures. Hence the prophetic looms large as an anti-Scriptural movement. It has become so epidemic; a false prophet was celebrated inside the Movement for rewriting the Scriptures changing thousands of passages because of a false Jesus took him into heaven and commissioned him to do so. Today false prophets are inside the Prophetic Movement and have been exposed by all their failed and false predictions. Yet are celebrated as God's prophets.

Ephesians 4:11-16
11 And he gave some, apostles; and some, prophets; an d some, evangelists; and some, pastors andteachers;

12 For the perfecting of the saints, for the work of the ministry, for the edifying of the body of Christ
13 Till we all come in the unity of the faith, and of the knowledge of the Son of God, unto perfect
man, unto the measure of the stature of the fulness of Christ:
14 That we henceforth be no more children, tossed to and fro, and carried about with every wind of
doctrine, by the sleight of men, and cunning craftiness, whereby they lie in wait to deceive;
15 But speaking the truth in love, may grow
up into him in all things, which is the head, even Christ:
16 From whom the whole body fitly joined
together and compacted by that
which every joint supplieth, according to the effectual working in the measure of
every part, maketh increase of the body unto the edifying of itself in love.

Corrupted Fruit
Perhaps the Church is having difficulty seeing the kind of harvest which is being produced today. As the Scriptures warn of a corrupted harvest, the Church needs to be vigilant in testing the fruit. It is one of Satan's master plans to sow corrupted seed right in with the good seed, so the corrupted fruit grows up right alongside of the good fruit. The Parable of the Wheat and Tares reveals this kind of spiritual warfare, which exists right inside the Church. Satan began to sow the corrupted seed with false apostles and prophets right in

the very beginning of the first century Church. Today's Church often acts like it is an offense against God to expose ministers who are sowing corrupted seeds, and who produce a corrupted harvest. All kinds of rules and boundaries have been set in place to "protect a corrupted minster."

According to Jesus how is one to detect a false prophet? The problem exists when you "follow the prophets signs and wonders," without testing the "seed he is sowing." The prophet's ministry by its very nature is based upon supernatural power, especially in revelatory gifting. However, the prophet is held in check by the Written Word of God and cannot move outside of the boundary of what has already been written. The prophet does not have any "seed coming from himself," instead the incorruptible seed which the prophet must sow "only comes from God's written word." The incorruptible seed is the Word of God which lives and abides forever. The Gospel was already determined before the formation of the world, as Jesus Christ is the Lamb of God slain before the foundation of the world. Gods Gospel is eternal, the incorruptible seed produces the harvest of "born again sons and daughters."

The corrupted seed is the "false gospel," it is a mixture of "half-truths," looks like the authentic Gospel but produces a corrupted fruit. The fruit which has been corrupted looks good on the outside, but on the inside upon greater examination it is rotten to the core. Jesus

Christ did not say there would be "no fruit," instead he said the fruit produced would be corrupted "evil fruit." Popularity, and success by the world's standards, large crowds, with abundant speaking platforms "are not the measure of a God given harvest." The seed sown, "the Gospel message," the incorruptible seed, the preaching of the Cross, Jesus Christ and Him crucified, is the message which is the unadulterated Gospel.

Not what is the problem with famous high visible preachers today? They cannot be rich and famous; they cannot have big crowds by "preaching the Cross." So, they have gone "to another Gospel," to put it bluntly the have gone to "Satan's Gospel." The men sowing it look charming, funny, gifted in speaking, can draw big audiences. However, the seed sown is "another gospel," which makes them false apostles and prophets. The harvest they say is so great Is "corrupted seed, a counterfeit, doctrines of demons." In the end it will produce a harvest of wickedness the worst being "counterfeited sons and daughters," who think they are following God, but have rottenness in their lives. Today we are experiencing the "maturing harvest of wheat and tares," both are beginning to put on the full head of grain or weeds.

Do not think it strange by the acceleration of corrupted bad fruit. Also, the abundance of false prophets who are demonically inspired to preach doctrines of demons. Neither be dismayed by a counterfeit harvest of corrupted fruit which is being celebrated by false prophets and false revival, and the counterfeit work of the false Holy Spirit. Only heed the warning of apostasy and deception, as in the last days many shall depart from the faith having itching ears and will follow the wickedness of evil men and imposters. Who will wax worse and worse deceiving and being deceived? The apostles and prophets will be especially tempting as they will have an element of the supernatural in their ministries. However, the test will be actually simple as they do not preach Jesus Christ and Him crucified? Does their message always reveal the Cross and person of Jesus Christ? Or do they preach mixture, a corrupted gospel, a corrupted seed. As no man can preach a corrupted false gospel and produce anything but corrupted bad fruit.

Deuteronomy 22:9

9 Thou shalt not sow thy vineyard with divers' seeds: lest the fruit of thy seed which thou hast sown, and the fruit of thy vineyard, be defiled.

1 Peter 1:23

23 Being born again, not of corruptible seed, but of incorruptible, by the word of God, which liveth and abideth forever.

Matthew 12:33-34

33 Either make the tree good, and his fruit good; or else make the tree corrupt, and his fruit corrupt: for the tree is known by his fruit.

34 O generation of vipers, how can ye, being evil, speak good things? for out of the abundance of the heart the mouth speaketh.

Matthew 7:15-20
15 Beware of false prophets, which come to you in sheep's clothing, but inwardly they are ravening wolves.
16 Ye shall know them by their fruits. Do men gather grapes of thorns, or figs of thistles?
17 Even so every good tree bringeth forth good fruit; but a corrupt tree bringeth forth evil fruit.
18 A good tree cannot bring forth evil fruit, neither can a corrupt tree bring forth good fruit.
19 Every tree that bringeth not forth good fruit is hewn down and cast into the fire.
20 Wherefore by their fruits ye shall know them.

The Danger of Following Balaam the False Prophet

Today in the modern Charismatic Movement is the presence of false prophets. The kind of false prophets which fall into the category of being like Balaam, the madness of the prophet which God rebuked by Balaam's own donkey.

What are some of the characteristics we must watch for in modern day Balaam like false prophet.?
1) They walk after the flesh without the fear of the Lord. They have the lust of uncleanness, having eyes of adultery, cannot cease from sin. Use

their ministries of prophetic to beguile unstable souls inside the Church.

2) They are presumptuous, self-entitled, self-willed, and are a law unto themselves. Which means when they commit adultery and walk-in perversity while imagine themselves above the law and without correction. When confronted with their immoral behaviors are not afraid to rail against God's government, refusing to be corrected.

3) They count it a pleasure to live immorally right in the middle of the Church, and the love feasts of the Lord. They are spots, and blemishes on the body of Christ bringing much shame and reproach to the Lord. As the world mocks the hypocrisy of their immorality when their sins are brought to light.

4) Balaam the false prophet, is self-deceived and self-deluded, as he sports himself with his own deceiving, while they feast in the middle of genuine Christians who walk with the Lord. The false prophets are most effective right in the middle of the Church, among Christians whom he has manipulated with many vain words, and boastings.

5) In reality they are wells without water, have gone dry, where once the Spirit of the Lord had brought refusing water through their ministries. They are clouds of a storm, surrounding their lives is the presence of evil. However, it is the

kind of evil which appears appealing and seductive. Many chase after the false prophet, as they allure through the lusts of the flesh, and many wanton desires. Those who are clean can run from the false prophets, knowing the demonic power of seduction which they possess.

6) They love the wages of unrighteousness. A covetousness heart, hard as stone, seared by the hypocrisy of immorality, in dire pursuit of exploiting the body of Christ. Balaam would sell his soul for money and sex, and pervert the Church in the process.

7) They promise you liberty with great swelling words. Boasting of great revivals and moves of God, but they themselves are slaves to corruption. For by what a man is overcome by, the same is enslaved by.

8) The have become dogs and pigs in their corruption. For after escaping the corruption in the world by a genuine faith in Christ, they go back from the Lord being entangled again in a life of perversion. It would have been better to not have known the way and turn from the Lord. As a dog which returns to its own vomit, and a pig after being washed goes back to wallowing in the mud.

9) Their latter end is worse than their beginning. A great Judgement has come upon them for they have become reprobates. A gross danger of being judged by God unto the mist of darkness,

which is one of the severest judgments which a fallen Christian can receive.

Is it mercy to judge a man who has exhibited the same traits of Balaam the false prophet in the New Testament Church? If we love the body of Christ, we will heed the warning of false prophets, and expose their hypocrisy to the utmost. As it is an act of mercy upon the madness of the prophet himself.

2 Peter 2:9-22
9 The Lord knoweth how to deliver the godly out of temptations, and to reserve the unjust unto the day of judgment to be punished:
10 But chiefly them that walk after the flesh in the lust of uncleanness and despise government. Presumptuous are they, self-willed, they are not afraid to speak evil of dignities.
11 Whereas angels, which are greater in power and might, bring not railing accusation against them before the Lord.
12 But these, as natural brute beasts, made to be taken and destroyed, speak evil of the things that they understand not; and shall utterly perish in their own corruption.
13 And shall receive the reward of unrighteousness, as they that count it pleasure to riot in the daytime. Spots they are and blemishes, sporting themselves with their own deceivings while they feast with you.

14 Having eyes full of adultery, and that cannot cease from sin; beguiling unstable souls: an heart they have exercised with covetous practices; cursed children:

15 Which have forsaken the right way, and are gone astray, following the way of Balaam the son of Bosor, who loved the wages of unrighteousness.

16 But was rebuked for his iniquity: the dumb ass speaking with man's voice forbad the madness of the prophet.

17 These are wells without water, clouds that are carried with a tempest; to whom the mist of darkness is reserved for ever.

18 For when they speak great swelling words of vanity, they allure through the lusts of the flesh, through much wantonness, those that were clean escaped from them who live in error.

19 While they promise them liberty, they themselves are the servants of corruption: for of whom a man is overcome, of the same is he brought in bondage.

20 For if after they have escaped the pollutions of the world through the knowledge of the Lord and Saviour Jesus Christ, they are again entangled therein, and overcome, the latter end is worse with them than the beginning.

21 For it had been better for them not to have known the way of righteousness, than, after they have known it, to turn from the holy commandment delivered unto them.

22 But it is happened unto them according to the true proverb, The dog is turned to his own vomit again; and the sow that was washed to her wallowing in the mire.

The Prevailing Influence of False Teachers

Why do the Scriptures warn of apostasy in the last days, which is led by false teachers and their doctrines of demons? It is apparent the warning in those days would be denied, by reason of deception and the agreement of Christians with the false teachers. So, what is the problem, popular men who are celebrated by thousands of Christians are actually pawns used by evil spirits to sow false doctrines which come from the corrupted wisdom of the Kingdom of darkness.

The question which should be asked? How come it is so easy for evil spirits to invade the Church, deceiving so many Christians at the same time? One simple explanation is evil spirits are able to imitate the work of God. Where Christians are deceived into believing they are from God. Satan is the great imitator, one of his main methods of deception is to bring in the counterfeit so as to go undetected. The Scriptures warn Satan brings in "another Jesus," another Gospel, and a false Holy Spirit. It has proven the Charismatic Signs and Wonders Movement has become very susceptible to evil spirits imitating the Holy Spirit. The Charismatic teaching of the Church bringing "heaven coming to earth," is not found in Scriptures. Is a doctrine of demons, and has opened the door for evil spirits to bring "lying signs and wonders?"

The signs and wonders dead end in themselves and have no redeeming values. They are supernatural in nature as they come from the power of evil spirits. Ironically, the more the Signs and Wonders Movement openly allowed all manner of supernatural manifestations, the more the New Age Movement was brought into practice. Today inside the Movement, Christians openly teach astral travel, communication with the dead, fortune telling and tarot card reading. All these supernatural powers are declared to come from the Holy Spirit and are a recovery of psychic powers which have been stolen from the Church by the New Age. These supernatural phenomena are the evidence taught by the Signs and Wonders Movement heaven has invaded earth. However, none of these supernatural encounters are heaven coming to earth, instead are evil spirits hiding their presence behind "false doctrinal beliefs."

The Signs and Wonders heaven to earth Movement has been exposed many times in false demonic practices but refuses correction. Instead, a practice of undermining the Written Word of God has openly manifested. Some of the main teachers has come to believe they are "modern apostles, "who are of equal authority as the original twelve apostles. As the result of this belief, men in the Signs and Wonders Movement believe they have the calling to "bring new light from the Scriptures." This has resulted in modern apostles reinterpreting and rewriting the Scriptures. The belief is the Bible is not a closed book, is now unfolding to apostles with new interpretations. Apostles who bring modern doctrines which in reality are their own private revelations, in exchange for age old held doctrinal beliefs. This might be one of the most demonic practices, being practiced inside the Movement as it has led to the rewriting of hundreds of Scriptures. In the formation of a new heaven to earth Preterist Bible called the Passion Translation. In times past any Movement which changed the Scriptures to add their own philosophies in the Scriptures, the Church would label that Movement a Christian cult. Today, the Scriptures have lost their place of authority in the modern Church so modern apostles and prophets are considered great reformers, instead of agents of evil spirits and deceivers.

Modern apostles and prophets are put before the Scriptures which has opened the door to doctrines of demons and making them false seductive teachers. This is the state of the modern apostolic/prophetic Movement which has been in great denial about the presence of evil spirits and doctrines of demons inside the Movement. Ignoring the warnings of end time apostasy, they have become susceptible to end time antichrist warfare inside the Church. Instead of being mature in the things of the Spirit, Charismatics are displaying their immaturity and inability to truly know the difference from the Holy Spirit, and demonic counterfeits. The Movement is not an elite Movement of reformation, instead is the source of false teachers, false apostles, false prophets, and doctrines of demons. If allowed to continue in its current state, the Movement will become one of the great influences of leading the Church into end time apostasy.

2 Timothy 3

1 This know also, that in the last days perilous times shall come.

2 For men shall be lovers of their own selves, covetous, boasters, proud, blasphemers, disobedient to parents, unthankful, unholy,

3 Without natural affection, trucebreakers, false accusers, incontinent, fierce, despisers of those that are good,

4 Traitors, heady, high minded, lovers of pleasures more than lovers of God;

5 Having a form of godliness, but denying the power thereof: from such turn away.

6 For of this sort are they which creep into houses, and lead captive silly women laden with sins, led away with divers lusts,

7 Ever learning, and never able to come to the knowledge of the truth.

8 Now as Jannes and Jambres withstood Moses, so do these also resist the truth: men of corrupt minds, reprobate concerning the faith.

9 But they shall proceed no further: for their folly shall be manifest unto all men, as theirs also was.

10 But thou hast fully known my doctrine, manner of life, purpose, faith, longsuffering, charity, patience,

11 Persecutions, afflictions, which came unto me at Antioch, at Iconium, at Lystra; what persecutions I endured: but out of them all the Lord delivered me.

12 Yea, and all that will live godly in Christ Jesus shall suffer persecution.

13 But evil men and seducers shall wax worse and worse, deceiving, and being deceived.

14 But continue thou in the things which thou hast learned and hast been assured of, knowing of whom thou hast learned them;

15 And that from a child thou hast known the holy scriptures, which are able to make thee wise unto salvation through faith which is in Christ Jesus.

16 All scripture is given by inspiration of God, and is profitable for doctrine, for reproof, for correction, for instruction in righteousness:

17 That the man of God may be perfect, throughly furnished unto all good works.

Satan's False Gospel

Did you know one of the main tactics in spiritual warfare is Satan's attempt to get you to accept his imitation counterfeit as the authentic? The great imitation of God is going on today all over the world, and even in the Church. It is not what looks blatantly false or evil, it is what is evil hidden by the appearance of good and truthful. Satan has the false Trinity, the False Godhead, where the False Messiah is soon to appear, the Son of Perdition, the Antichrist. The Great Dragon himself seeks worship as God and sows the false prophets and messengers who proclaim the false Gospel. Did you know Satan has invaded the Church throughout the world by sowing another Jesus, and a false Gospel which leads the masses away from true worship of Jesus Christ?

Did you know the true Gospel appears to be foolish to the minds of men who are darkened in their understanding? The preaching of the Cross is an offense to the perishing, it appears as a foolish message. Did you also know the preaching of the False Gospel is very popular and draws the masses by the multiple millions into a false light and counterfeit salvation? Hundreds of millions of souls have been drawn into counterfeit religions, and religious organizations trapped and enslaved by the false Gospel. Why are so many drawn into the counterfeit if it were just a neutral situation? However, the Prince of the Power of the Air has designed the False Gospel as an imitation so as to keep men under the deception they serve God, so as not to expose Satan is right in their midst. How many are willing to give their lives to the Prince of Darkness under the delusion their false Gospel is Gods true message. Men and women who are led down the prime rose path only to wake up in the Fires of Hell seduced by the lies of a False Gospel. Satan works his tireless temptation to suppress the authentic Gospel of Jesus Christ with great swelling words of vanity, which deny the one and only true God and Great King, Jesus Christ. Why do you reject the message of the Cross? The answer is simple, you have accepted a counterfeit system of false beliefs which have originated from the Kingdom of Darkness.

The deception of the false Gospel runs deep in other religions, but what of the organized Church? Satan's master ploy is to sow the seeds of a corrupted Gospel right among the wheat, the Sons of God. Did you know the most popular Gospel inside the modern organized Church is the one which has minimized the Cross, and exalted man's ideas and philosophy in its place? Did you know the Bible predicts in the last days the false Gospel will be the message Christians run after? In fact, they will shut their ears to the message of the Cross refusing to submit their lives to Jesus Christ and will turn to Christian fables. The Church will seek after men who are willing to preach the false Gospel, Christian Fables, so as to have the ears itched by only being told what they want to hear. The problem will be so chronic they will heap for themselves the false prophets, the false apostles, the false teachers who carry another Gospel by another spirit. Which leads to another Jesus which is carried about by doctrines of demons and evil spirits.

We are already deep in those days! What is one of the greatest dangers of modern Christianity? To follow a man, a women who preaches an imitation Gospel which seduces the Church to follow an imitation Satanic Jesus. Will Christians know they are being deceived? Yes and no. Many will warn of the false apostles and false prophets which are in the pulpits. Many will use the Scriptures to expose the False Gospel and False Messengers. However, the seduction has come with Christians to ignore the Scriptures or even undermine the Scriptures through unbelief. In short, they will not take the Bible as their final authority and will not submit to the Scriptures in their literal teaching. As a Christian you can suppress the truth by manipulating the Scriptures to say something the original text does not say. The False Gospel is simply a manipulation of the Scriptures by putting a private interpretation of man's ideas and philosophy in its place. Satan is deep into the Church which has allowed men of fame and fortune to undermine the Gospel. Did know men who call themselves apostles and prophets have heartedly approved of the rewriting of Scriptures to manufacture an imitation Bible with their philosophical beliefs rewritten and infused into the Scriptures. Watch out for any Christian Movement that needs to rewrite the Bible to fit their narrative, and endorse they alone have the proper understanding of Scriptures. As these has already happened in the Charismatic Movement, one can only question is the Great Apostasy from the faith well underway ?Lead by Satan's end time False Gospel?

2 Timothy 4:1-5

1 I charge thee therefore before God, and the Lord
Jesus Christ, who shall judge the quick and the dead at
his appearing and his kingdom.
2 Preach the word; be instant in season, out of season;
reprove, rebuke, exhort with all longsuffering and
doctrine.
3 For the time will come when they will not endure
sound doctrine; but after their own lusts shall they heap
to themselves teachers, having itching ears; 4 And they
shall turn away their ears from the truth, and shall be
turned unto fables.
5 But watch thou in all things, endure afflictions, do the
work of an evangelist, make full proof of thy ministry.

Conclusion

Works of Flesh and Kingdom Exclusion

Many Christians are surprised to find out they can be
disqualified from the Kingdom of Heaven, the coming
Millennial Kingdom. However, Jesus Christ warned His
disciples of Kingdom exclusion as well as many of the
Apostolic writers of the New Testament.

Matthew 7:21-23

21 Not everyone that saith unto me, Lord, Lord, shall
enter into the kingdom of heaven; but he that doeth the
will of my Father which is in heaven.
22 Many will say to me in that day, Lord, Lord, have we
not prophesied in thy name? and in thy name have cast

out devils? and in thy name done many wonderful works?

23 And then will I profess unto them, I never knew you: depart from me, ye that work iniquity.

Notice in this passage those who are being shut out from entering the Kingdom appear to be Christians who used the things of God in an iniquitous way. Depart from Me you workers of iniquity for I never knew you is the Judgment Christ uses on these disciples. A disqualification not based upon never being born again, instead a judgment of works after coming into saving faith. What is being judged are works of righteousness, some are declared as wood, hay, and stubble and are burned up in Christ's judicial fires. The fire burns up as the fleshly works, leaving only the person's eternal life, so the come out smelling like smoke but the soul is saved.

Notice how the apostle Paul gives the same warning to Christians of Kingdom disqualification, when works of the flesh are practiced. The Kingdom age is not automatically given by the Cross, even though eternal salvation is given. The loss is to be "disinherited at the Judgment Seat," judged for the works of the flesh, and shut out from the Kingdom age as a form of judgment and discipline.

Galatians 5:19-21
19 Now the works of the flesh are manifest, which are these, Adultery, fornication, uncleanness, lasciviousness,
20 Idolatry, witchcraft, hatred, variance, emulations, wrath, strife, seditions, heresies,
21 Envyings, murders, drunkenness, revellings, and such like: of the which I tell you before, as I have also told you in time past, that they which do such things shall not inherit the kingdom of God.

Notice how living in the flesh after you are born again causes the loss of the Kingdom age. Living a sexually immoral life, or sexual uncleanness will be judged at the Judgment Seat leading to disinherited judgment. You will be considered a reprobate, disqualified from the inheritance. Paul called the Kingdom Age the prize of the high calling, which he was running in a race of faith to qualify. If Paul did not bring his body under subjection, Paul would be a reprobate from being crowned and losing the right to rule and reign with Christ in the Kingdom age.

Also notice the other works of the flesh which disqualify the saints from Kingdom inheritance. Those who bring strife, sedition's, and heresies are included. Is it not amazing those highly celebrated Christians who teach doctrines of demons will be disqualified from the Kingdom age, by teaching heresies which divide the body of Christ? Getting in the flesh and excusing yourself under the banner of grace will not work at the Judgment Seat of Christ.

Christians who get in the flesh, who like to get high, or drunk, or any other addiction will give an account at the Judgment Seat. What Christians do now after coming into saving faith really matters, as our lives will qualify or disqualify us for the next age. Many passages warn Christian they can forfeit their right of first-born sons and sell out their birth rights to the Kingdom age for the pleasures of sin in this age. If Christians say a man or woman born of the Spirit can lose their eternal life and go to Hell after coming into saving faith, the reason is unconfessed sin and ungodly living. However, the Scriptures do prove the Kingdom can be disinherited for these very same reasons. Which shuts ungodly disciples from entering the Kingdom of Heaven in comparison of going to Hell. Kingdom disqualification is not the same thing as going to Hell, as even the apostle Paul warned he could be disqualified, a reprobate after years of suffering for Christ, and writing many portions of the New Testament. Kingdom disqualification is one thing related to Christians based upon works of righteousness or works of the flesh. Where an eternity in Hell is a judgment upon unbelievers who have refused Christ.

We must learn not to go beyond Scriptures, the loss of the Kingdom is clearly given. Even if one were to believe Christians can go to Hell and lose their salvation. The must admit the loss of the Kingdom does not mean

Christians have been sent to Hell. It simply means they are disqualified from the rewards of entering into the next age, to rule with Christ for 1000 years.

1 Corinthians 6:8-10
8 Nay, ye do wrong, and defraud, and that your brethren.
9 Know ye not that the unrighteous shall not inherit the kingdom of God? Be not deceived: neither fornicators, nor idolaters, nor adulterers, nor effeminate, nor abusers of themselves with mankind,
10 Nor thieves, nor covetous, nor drunkards, nor revilers, nor extortioners, shall inherit the kingdom of God.

Ephesians 5:1-7
1 Be ye therefore followers of God, as dear children.
2 And walk in love, as Christ also hath loved us, and hath given himself for us an offering and a sacrifice to God for a sweet-smelling savour.
3 But fornication, and all uncleanness, or covetousness, let it not be once named among you, as becometh saints;
4 Neither filthiness, nor foolish talking, nor jesting, which are not convenient: but rather giving of thanks.
5 For this ye know, that no whoremonger, nor unclean person, nor covetous man, who is an idolater, hath any inheritance in the kingdom of Christ and of God.

6 Let no man deceive you with vain words: for because of these things cometh the wrath of God upon the children of disobedience.

7 Be not ye therefore partakers with them.

2 Peter 1:8-11

8 For if these things be in you, and abound, they make you that ye shall neither be barren nor unfruitful in the knowledge of our Lord Jesus Christ.

9 But he that lacketh these things is blind, and cannot see afar off, and hath forgotten that he was purged from his old sins.

10 Wherefore the rather, brethren, give diligence to make your calling and election sure: for if ye do these things, ye shall never fall:

11 For so an entrance shall be ministered unto you abundantly into the everlasting kingdom of our Lord and Saviour Jesus Christ.

House Built Upon the Rock

Matthew the 7:24-29

24 Therefore whosoever heareth these sayings of mine, and doeth them, I will liken him unto a wiseman, which built his house upon a rock:

25 And the rain descended, and the floods came, and the winds blew, and beat upon that house; and it fell not: for it was founded upon a rock.

26 And every one that heareth these sayings of

mine, and doeth them not, shall be likened a
foolish man, which built his house upon the sand:
27 And the rain descended, and the
floods came, and the winds blew, and beat
upon that house; and it fell: and great was the fall of it.
28 And it came to pass, when Jesus had
ended these sayings, the people were astonished at his
doctrine:
29 For he taught them as one having authority, and not
as the scribes.

The Lord ends the Sermon On the Mount with a
contrast between two disciples. The difference will be
with all the Disciples of the Lord who hear the Sermon
On the Mount following the teachings and commands
resident within. Or those who are also the Disciples of
Jesus Christ but fail to act upon the teachings and
commands. The contrast then is broken down between
the two disciples.
The first hears the teachings and commands of Jesus
Christ and does them. The Lord likens this disciple to a
wiseman who is building a house and is wise enough to
consider the foundation of the house. The foundation
must be solid enough to endure the conditions which
will come. The wise man builds his house upon the rock
which Scriptures reveal is Jesus Christ Himself.
Matthew 16:15-18
15 He saith unto them, But whom say ye that I am?
16 And Simon Peter answered and said, Thou art the
Christ, the Son of the living God

17 And Jesus answered and said unto him, Blessed art thou, Simon Bar–
jona: for flesh and bloodhath not revealed it unto thee, but my Father which is in heaven.
18 And I say also unto
thee, That thou art Peter, and upon this rock I will build my church; and the gates of hell shall not prevail against it.

The Church of Jesus Christ is founded upon the revelation of Jesus Christ as the Son of God, and the head of the Church. As the Head of the body of Christ, disciples of Jesus Christ must obey Christ according to His commands and teachings. The Sermon On the Mount has laid down the commands which will determine future rewards based upon judgments at the Second Coming of Jesus Christ. The promise in Matthew chapter sixteen demonstrates Jesus Christ has the power over the future resurrection of all men. For the righteous the resurrection of rewards, and qualification into ruling with Jesus Christ into the Kingdom of Heaven age. For the unrighteous a resurrection one thousand years after the first resurrection. The resurrection of the wicked is out from Hades, Hell and into the Lake of Fire for all eternity. The wiseman has be warned of the reality of eternal judgment. For the wise in this life live forward towards the Second Coming, and eternal life in Christ.

Now what of the wise and foolish virgins? Are they not all virgins seeking the Lord's favor? Wanting to partake in the Marriage Supper of the Lamb. Five were wise and had enough oil to go the whole way finding entrance into the Marriage Supper. Five were foolish, and the door into the Marriage Supper was shut on them. Jesus Christ would not recognize the five foolish virgins as the Bride of Christ. Perhaps, the real story can be found in the Sermon On the Mount in the separation between wise and foolish disciples.

The wise Disciple of Jesus Christ heard the sayings of Jesus Christ and acted upon them living by these commands during their lifetimes. The wise man considered the storms and trials which would beset all men. Those who are able to preserve through the storms of life are those who built their lives upon the commands and teachings of Jesus Christ. As the words of Jesus Christ are the eternal infallible Word of God which cannot be corrupted or fade away. A wise disciple has built his house upon the words of Jesus Christ and can withstand the storms which threaten to destroy it.

Notice the storms come to both the wise and foolish in the same manner. "25 And the rain descended, and the floods came, and the winds blew, and beat upon that house; and it fell not: for it was founded upon a rock." The difference between the wise and foolish disciple is how the built their lives upon the words of Jesus Christ. Beyond the initial experience of being born again, into a sanctified life following the commands of the Sermon On the Mount. The life of the wise disciple has the foundation of the rock of Jesus Christ.

The foolish man also being a disciple hears the sayings of Jesus Christ but will not build his future upon acting upon those commands. When the same trials come, rains descend, floods arise, and winds blow, and beat upon the house and great was the fall of it. Seems not just light damage which can be recovered instead irreversible damage in which the house is lost. If we try to apply this parable to men who are not saved, the answer is obvious as they never intended to obey Jesus Christ in the first place. If we place this parable with Disciples of Jesus Christ, the wise being those who obey seeing growth into Christ likeness, and the foolish who disobey and do not mature in Christ. The Great fall of the house of the foolish disciple represents the loss of Kingdom age rewards, and failure to enter the Kingdom age. Just like Jesus Christ has just warned in a few passages before this parable.

"28 And it came to pass, when Jesus had
ended these sayings, the people were astonished at his doctrine:
29 For he taught them as one having authority, and not as the scribes."

The effects of the commands, doctrine, and warnings of the Sermon On the Mount brings about great conviction upon all who hear. Never has there been a man who spoke with such authority, who words are eternal. No man can just walk away treating the Sermon On the Mount in a casual matter. It demands a man's life full attention and surrender. For all who refuse the sayings of Jesus Christ will stand before the Lord and are without excuse.